THE BEDFORD SERIES IN HISTORY AND CULTURE

The American Women's Movement, 1945–2000

A Brief History with Documents

Related Titles in
THE BEDFORD SERIES IN HISTORY AND CULTURE
Advisory Editors: Lynn Hunt, *University of California, Los Angeles*
David W. Blight, *Yale University*
Bonnie G. Smith, *Rutgers University*
Natalie Zemon Davis, *Princeton University*
Ernest R. May, *Harvard University*

THE BEDFORD SERIES IN HISTORY AND CULTURE

The American Women's Movement, 1945–2000

A Brief History with Documents

Nancy MacLean

Duke University

BEDFORD/ST. MARTIN'S   Boston ◆ New York

For Bedford/St. Martin's

Publisher for History: Mary V. Dougherty
Director of Development for History: Jane Knetzger
Senior Editor: Heidi L. Hood
Developmental Editor: Kathryn Abbott
Editorial Assistant: Katherine Flynn
Senior Production Supervisor: Nancy J. Myers
Production Associate: Samuel Jones
Executive Marketing Manager: Jenna Bookin Barry
Text Design: Claire Seng-Niemoeller
Project Management: Books By Design, Inc.
Index: Books By Design, Inc.
Cover Design: Joy Lin
Cover Photo: The Last Mile for the Torch Relay from Seneca Falls to Houston for the Opening of the First National Women's Conference, 1977. Image includes Sylvia Ortiz, Peggy Kokernot, and Michele Cearcy. © Diana Mara Henry/dianamarahenry.com.
Composition: TexTech International
Printing and Binding: RR Donnelley & Sons Company

President: Joan E. Feinberg
Editorial Director: Denise B. Wydra
Director of Marketing: Karen R. Soeltz
Director of Editing, Design, and Production: Marcia Cohen
Assistant Director of Editing, Design, and Production: Elise S. Kaiser
Manager, Publishing Services: Emily Berleth

Library of Congress Control Number: 2008923371

Manufactured in the United States of America.

7 6 5 4
l k j i h

For information, write: Bedford/St. Martin's, 75 Arlington Street, Boston, MA 02116   (617-399-4000)

ISBN-10: 0-312-44801-5
ISBN-13: 978-0-312-44801-1

Acknowledgments

Acknowledgments and copyrights are continued at the back of the book on pages 188–90, which constitute an extension of the copyright page.

Distributed outside North America by PALGRAVE MACMILLAN.

Foreword

The Bedford Series in History and Culture is designed so that readers can study the past as historians do.

The historian's first task is finding the evidence. Documents, letters, memoirs, interviews, pictures, movies, novels, or poems can provide facts and clues. Then the historian questions and compares the sources. There is more to do than in a courtroom, for hearsay evidence is welcome, and the historian is usually looking for answers beyond act and motive. Different views of an event may be as important as a single verdict. How a story is told may yield as much information as what it says.

Along the way the historian seeks help from other historians and perhaps from specialists in other disciplines. Finally, it is time to write, to decide on an interpretation and how to arrange the evidence for readers.

Each book in this series contains an important historical document or group of documents, each document a witness from the past and open to interpretation in different ways. The documents are combined with some element of historical narrative—an introduction or a biographical essay, for example—that provides students with an analysis of the primary source material and important background information about the world in which it was produced.

Each book in the series focuses on a specific topic within a specific historical period. Each provides a basis for lively thought and discussion about several aspects of the topic and the historian's role. Each is short enough (and inexpensive enough) to be a reasonable one-week assignment in a college course. Whether as classroom or personal reading, each book in the series provides firsthand experience of the challenge—and fun—of discovering, recreating, and interpreting the past.

Lynn Hunt
David W. Blight
Bonnie G. Smith
Natalie Zemon Davis
Ernest R. May

Preface

The modern women's movement transformed the United States for both sexes, fundamentally altering the lives of millions of people. From education, employment, politics, and religion to child rearing, sexuality, leisure, and personal relationships, no facet of American life was untouched by feminism and the grassroots activism of the 1960s and 1970s that shaped it. Living in a very different era, today's students often find it difficult to understand how such sweeping changes occurred. The introduction and documents in *The American Women's Movement, 1945–2000: A Brief History with Documents* will equip them to answer some important historical questions: What made so many women receptive to feminism in the late 1960s? Why did this mass movement arise in the 1960s and 1970s and not earlier? How did a minority manage to persuade the majority of the need for significant changes? How did women activists, despite being underrepresented in the political establishment, manage to move Congress, the courts, and several presidents to enact reforms? How have their victories and the resultant changes in culture affected others, including the young women and men of today?

A study of the women's movement not only reveals an essential part of recent American history, but it also provides the opportunity to learn about how citizens achieve significant change. An examination of feminist activism demonstrates how bottom-up pressure from the grassroots interacted in complex ways with top-down action from the nation's power centers to produce meaningful reforms. These reforms have improved the quality of life of millions of Americans and made the country more inclusive and democratic.

The introduction and the documents that follow defy static categorization: liberal feminism, radical feminism, socialist feminism, black feminism, and so on. Rather, the introduction highlights the connections between the women's movement and other reform struggles from 1945 to 2000, most notably the labor movement and civil rights. Paying particular attention to the variety of feminist activists and to the responses of their opponents, the introduction seeks to dispel the misconception that the American women's movement was simply a white, middle-class cause. Further, the introduction traces the evolution of the women's movement from the second wave to the more recent third wave.

Organized chronologically to give students a sense of change over time, the documents reproduced in this book capture the historical depth and social breadth of the movement. The collection begins with the grievances and resources American women had accumulated by the end of World War II, and then charts how women activists launched new organizations and redirected old ones, identified and debated issues, elaborated visions, developed policies, listened to critics, built powerful bonds around the globe, and modified their agendas as they navigated obstacles and expanded their ranks over several decades, especially during the 1960s, 1970s, and 1980s. The documents chosen engage the concerns of today's students, such as work and family balance, social justice, and sexuality. Also included are select documents from those who opposed the women's movement. Document headnotes situate individual documents within the context of race, class, age, religion, and geography.

The appendixes offer additional helpful resources. The chronology provides a sequence of important events to help students better understand causation and consequences. The questions for consideration invite analysis of the dynamics of women's activism and synthesis of information into meaningful patterns. The bibliography guides readers to important scholarship. Much remains to be learned about the women's movement in the last half-century, and the readers of this book will find a solid introduction from which to explore the impact of American history and the women's movement on their own lives.

ACKNOWLEDGMENTS

I am grateful to many people for their contributions to this work. At Bedford/St. Martin's, I thank Patricia Rossi for her enthusiasm at the start of this book, Mary Dougherty for being its champion thereafter, Jane Knetzger and Katherine Flynn for help with queries along the way, and Emily Berleth and Nancy Benjamin for their production expertise. I especially appreciate the deep knowledge, wise judgment, and excellent suggestions of development editor Kathryn Abbott and the external readers, Danielle Alexander of Napa Valley College; Jennifer

Brier of the University of Illinois–Chicago; Nan Enstad of the University of Wisconsin; Linda Gordon of New York University; Paula Hinton of Tennessee Technological University; and Karen Manners Smith of Emporia State University. A huge thank-you to all of them and also to Jarod Roll, Hunter Thomson, and Tony Abata for superb research assistance, and to Ronnie Grinberg, Kate Nestler, Mike Sherry, and Lane Fenrich for help with images and sources. I owe special gratitude to Paula Blaskovits, without whose unrivaled competence, commitment, and good cheer in the face of onrushing trains I could never have completed this book. I thank Bruce Orenstein for making all things better, from first drafts to everyday life.

This book owes its existence and much about its approach to the outstanding teachers from whom I learned women's history. I am grateful to Mari Jo Buhle, my senior thesis adviser, and Linda Gordon, my dissertation adviser, for being such inspiring mentors and supportive colleagues. I especially want to thank Gerda Lerner for creating the first doctoral program in American women's history at the University of Wisconsin–Madison in 1982. Her vision of and dedication to women's history attracted an extraordinary group of students to Madison, and her organizing talent and sheer hard work kept us fed and writing. From that then-risky experiment, the program's students have become lifelong friends and intellectual interlocutors, teaching one another more than words can express through example, challenge, and solidarity. This book is dedicated to all the participants in that thriving community.

                                                    Nancy MacLean

Contents

APPENDIXES

Illustrations

THE BEDFORD SERIES IN HISTORY AND CULTURE

The American Women's Movement, 1945–2000

A Brief History with Documents

PART ONE

Introduction:
The Movement That
Changed a Nation

Nothing like it had happened before in the United States. Twenty thousand people gathered to discuss the problems women faced and propose ways to solve them at the National Women's Conference held in Houston, Texas, on November 18–21, 1977. Over two thousand of the attendees were delegates who had been elected by conventions held in every state of the Union, in which 130,000 participants shaped the agenda. The nation had never seen a more diverse representative assembly. More than a third of the delegates were women of color, and one in five had grown up in poverty. The delegates produced a National Plan of Action with twenty-six planks calling for reforms on a wide range of issues. They called for high-quality, low-cost child care, equal treatment in the workplace, Social Security for homemakers, an increase in the minimum wage, an end to discrimination against women of color and lesbians, protection for battered women, an end to legal rape in marriage, vocational training for women in prison, reproductive freedom, better representation of women in the media and the arts, and the passage of an Equal Rights Amendment to the U.S. Constitution.

Why did this vast and diverse group gather together, and what made them so bold? Twenty years before, such an assemblage would have been unimaginable. As late as 1971, polls found that a majority of the public opposed "efforts to strengthen and change women's status in society." Yet, by 1975, 63 percent of Americans supported women's equality, and Congress responded to that new enthusiasm by passing a law calling for the Houston conference. What caused this rapid turnaround?

THE IMPACT OF ACTIVISM

It happened because a massive social movement demanded change and organized to win it. As this grassroots struggle gave voice to diverse groups of women, it provided a vocabulary to address issues that had once been inexpressible. Movement participants issued manifestos, held discussions, pressured politicians, filed lawsuits, organized demonstrations, and sponsored "speak outs." Above all, they built coalitions with others who shared some of their values and goals. Beginning with small numbers of self-described "feminists" in 1966 and 1967, the movement soon enlisted the energies of tens of thousands of women and men. Their efforts to achieve fairness reached into every corner of the country and every nook of daily life. Ideas and habits long treated as common sense came under scrutiny as never before, as activists questioned and altered the country's institutions: families, schools, workplaces, religions, government, and cultural institutions. Thanks to their efforts, the most basic parts of life became more democratic—among them, love, work, faith, sex, education, and child raising.

Throughout the country, what would have been unthinkable fifty years ago is now taken for granted. From advertising to zookeeping, women are now employed in occupations that would have excluded them before. Women now serve as decorated officers in the armed forces, as star athletes who are cheered by both men and women, and as conduits to the divine in a growing number of religious denominations. Today, a majority of married women are in the labor force, most of them because they must work to support their families. In organizing their lives around the expectation of lifelong employment, they seek advanced education in record numbers, and they have made marriage more fulfilling for both partners. Men are doing more hands-on child rearing and housework than ever before, as growing numbers of them have come to appreciate equality in marriage. Violence against women—once treated as fodder by comedians and regularly ignored by police—is now taken seriously. Women who are victims of battering, rape, and incest can find public sympathy and support services. Lesbians and gay men, hounded from federal jobs for their sexuality in the 1950s, now serve as legislators, out and proud, with devoted constituents of all orientations. Backed by Title IX's guarantee of equal access to sports, young women are growing up with a novel sense of their physical power. All of this has happened because ordinary women, at first in small numbers, took seriously the promise of democracy and used their civil rights, as the Houston delegates summarized their hope, "to form a more perfect Union."

These changes arrived with such dizzying speed and variety that to some observers, it seemed they had materialized out of thin air. People imagined the movement as a veritable force of nature—an "eruption" or "tidal wave" of that "explosive" era—the 1960s. Seeking to provide some context, the media spoke of a "revival" or "reawakening" of the women's movement, ultimately of the "second wave" of a feminism that had presumably slumbered since winning the vote in 1920. But the roots of the new movement ran deep, making possible the coalitions that produced so many stunning victories in quick succession. The cause that became front-page news in the late 1960s had been under way for well over a century. Its potential to become a mass, effective movement grew from the reform infrastructure built during the Progressive Era and the New Deal period; the demand for a larger and more skilled labor pool generated by World War II, the cold war, and the postwar consumer economy; and the inspiration and training provided by the labor movement, the civil rights movement, and the New Left of the 1950s and 1960s. These influences enabled an initially small group to find ways to move hundreds of thousands and to effect significant change.

THE LONG WOMEN'S MOVEMENT

For over a century and a half, activity on behalf of women's equality among at least a small minority of women had been nearly constant. Typically, as in the 1960s, feminism emerged from wider social reform. As activist women acquired the ideas, tools, and confidence to seek change for other causes, many came to see gender injustice with fresh eyes—and then learned in short order that few of their male comrades took it as seriously as they did. In 1837, the radical Quaker abolitionist, antiracist, and self-made intellectual Sarah Grimké became the first American to write a full-length feminist treatise. She appealed to "our brethren" to "take their feet from off our necks, and permit us to stand upright on that ground which God designed us to occupy."[1] Her work helped inspire those who organized the first women's rights conference in Seneca Falls, New York, in 1848. From the time they declared that "all men AND WOMEN are created equal" and vowed that a woman should know no "master" but her own conscience, varied groups of women came together to work for justice for their sex.

A tiny minority before the Civil War, feminists held women's rights conventions to work toward what they called "co-equality" with men. They developed their analysis and vision in debates over every question pertaining to their lives, from married women's status, to education, to women's place in church, professions, and community, to divorce and more. Using the language of republicanism and liberalism, they identified the ways that culture, law, religion, and everyday habit conspired to restrain women.

Following the Civil War, in the era known as the Gilded Age, the seed produced by earlier activism germinated in a nationwide campaign for voting rights for women. But feminists divided over how to seek suffrage. Some, led by Elizabeth Cady Stanton and Susan B. Anthony, created the National Woman Suffrage Association, which sought rights for women like themselves (propertied, native born, and white), even at the expense of other victims of discrimination. Outraged that male former slaves and male immigrants new to the country were granted rights denied to them, Stanton and Anthony's organization allied with racist and nativist politicians in hopes of persuading the overwhelmingly white, native-born male electorate to support woman suffrage. Other feminists, remaining loyal to their abolitionist allies, prioritized votes for black men, while continuing to seek equality for women in other ways. Led by Lucy Stone and others, they built the American Woman Suffrage Association and worked closely with the Republican Party in support of Reconstruction. That fundamental difference over whom feminism should advance and how the cause should relate to wider efforts at social justice would resound through later generations, as activists divided by race and class in particular.

In the meantime, many women's groups worked to better the whole society and improve women's status in the process. Hundreds of thousands participated in the Women's Christian Temperance Union and the General Federation of Women's Clubs. Others worked in the National Association of Colored Women, the Knights of Labor, the Populist movement, the American Federation of Labor, the settlement house movement, antilynching campaigns, and other organizing efforts. Collectively, their action showed that the debate was no longer over *whether* women should participate in public life but over *how* and toward what ends.

In the 1910s, some astute organizers saw how women's diversity could be a source of strength. They transformed the campaign for woman suffrage by recruiting reformers from an array of causes who sought the vote to advance their goals, among them settlement house workers, labor activists, and radical advocates of birth control. These new groups' techniques—picketing, demonstrations, and flamboyant parades—endowed the suffrage struggle with mass appeal and attracted large numbers of college-age women. Gaining ground in the 1910s, the suffragists won the Nineteenth Amendment to the U.S. Constitution in 1920. A seventy-year struggle had at last gained U.S. women the right to vote.

After ratification, some women dropped out, but the most committed activists continued to work for change. A minority of self-described "feminists" joined Alice Paul and the National Women's Party to work for an Equal Rights Amendment that would make U.S. law and public policy gender-blind and thus open new opportunities to women. Most others, however, saw such gender-blindness as a danger to less-privileged women, who stood to lose protective laws for women in industry and economic security if gender-conscious reform measures were outlawed. These women devoted themselves instead to wider social reform, working through the labor movement, the League of Women Voters, and other liberal and radical organizations. Their efforts expanded during the New Deal years, when women assumed policy-making positions in record numbers as part of a national female reform network anchored by the Women's Bureau of the Labor Department.

When the United States went to war against Germany, Italy, and Japan in 1941, the government turned to women to fill the jobs created by wartime production. Policymakers put pressure on employers to hire women for traditionally male jobs and invited women to take advantage of new opportunities. The number of women in the workforce suddenly doubled, as did the number of employed wives. In all, 6 million new women entered the labor force, and others found better-paying jobs and received recognition for advancing the war effort. Another 350,000 women contributed more directly by joining the military. As significant as the cultural challenge to old gender norms was the partial breakdown of occupational race and sex segregation. Black women, like black men, got better jobs than ever before, as they escaped the cotton fields and domestic service for newly opened, better-paying positions in unionized manufacturing. Overall, female union membership quadrupled. These women laid the foundation for a feminist movement through networks that promoted working women's interests.

Thanks to the Allied victory in the hard-fought war, in 1945 millions of Americans felt a kind of collective efficacy that later generations would find hard to imagine. As a new United Nations arose to ensure that the horrors of world war would never be repeated, progressive Americans believed that economic security, social justice, and world peace were within humanity's grasp. The sense of a historic opportunity to construct a better world led a group of women to set about building the Congress of American Women (CAW) in 1946. CAW attracted a broad range of women who had remained active for women's equality and social reform after the passage of the Nineteenth Amendment. An umbrella group, it brought together left-wing activists, progressive labor unionists, liberals, civil rights activists, peace workers, and European ethnic groups (see Document 1).

These activists created an agenda for gender justice that involved gaining equal education, ending job segregation and wage discrimination, reforming the nation's laws, improving the image of women in the media, and addressing the particular discrimination that minority women experienced. They also pointed to women's sole responsibility for housework as a serious problem, especially for employed women who came home from the job to a "double day" of work at home (see Document 2). CAW organized under the banner of human rights and world peace, which had wide appeal in the wake of fascism, the Holocaust, and the bombing of Hiroshima and Nagasaki. The commitment to human rights was evident when CAW made racial equality central to its program and featured more black women in leadership positions than any other feminist or peace movement in U.S. history.

THE CHILLING EFFECTS OF THE RED SCARE

Yet within a few years, the national political climate shifted from hope to fear as the cold war commenced. Even the seasoned organizers of CAW found that they were no match for a government gearing up for world conflict and determined to crush dissent with all the many powers at its disposal. CAW had built a broad coalition, but Communist women played a key role in bringing it together. They maintained ties to the Communist-led Women's International Democratic Federation abroad and organized against nuclear weapons, which proved to be their Achilles' heel when the cold war heated up in 1947 and the United States and the Soviet Union became bitter enemies.

Both at home and abroad, American officials turned against radicals—often labeled "reds"—with a vengeance. The House Un-American Activities Committee (HUAC) targeted CAW in 1948, frightening away many liberal supporters. In 1950, the U.S. attorney general ordered the group to register as a foreign enemy agent, an untenable position for CAW. If they agreed to the slanderous designation and registered, they would be inviting a death sentence; if they resisted, the organization would end up bankrupt, with its leaders possibly incarcerated. Fear of such reprisal intimidated activists. Membership plummeted from a claimed high of 250,000 to 3,000. Throughout the United States, the repression of radicalism created a forbidding climate for organizing for gender equality just as it did for the labor and civil rights movements. By the mid-1950s, calling for world peace and racial justice made a person vulnerable to suspicion, harassment, and unemployment.

Indeed, the Red Scare halted much of U.S. women's progress by equating work for social justice and disarmament with Communist subversion. Fear of being tarred as Communist led the labor movement to purge its most progressive unions, among them a cannery workers' union that enrolled large numbers of Latinas with a labor-based feminist vision and an electrical workers' union at the cutting edge of the fight for gender equity on the job. The Red Scare also prevented expansion of New Deal programs to include national health care and ended hopes for extending basic benefits to farm and domestic workers—two leading occupations of African Americans and Mexican Americans at the time. That impasse led to deepening race and gender inequality.

In culture, as in foreign and domestic policy, the motto of American leaders became "containment," including containing challenges to gender hierarchy. When the majority of women employed during the war insisted on keeping their jobs after it ended (80 percent of those over age forty-five did), they were assailed with magazine articles like "I Denied My Sex," warning of the terrible consequences of denying one's feminine nature by pursuing a career or entering politics. And many "experts"—from psychologists to sociologists to school guidance counselors—agreed. Their arguments struck a chord among millions of women and men who had endured fifteen years of loss, fear, and deprivation during the Great Depression and the war. The pent-up desire for the pleasures of family life contributed to the stunning birthrate that produced the baby-boom generation and fueled the postwar consumer economy.

Yet even in the chilly political climate of the 1950s, tens of thousands of women continued to be active in public life, working for wider goals with special attention to women's needs. They operated beneath the radar of a media obsessed with the sharply polarized gender roles of the white suburban ideal. One example was Church Women United, an ecumenical group founded in 1941 with representatives from seventy Protestant denominations. Its members sought to live out their faith by seeking justice and peace through service. Other women were active in mixed-sex liberal groups, such as the American Civil Liberties Union and the Quaker-based American Friends Service Committee, or in mainstream women's organizations, such as the League of Women Voters. Still others focused on international problems, such as Women's Strike for Peace, founded in 1961 (see Document 6).

The women activists of the 1950s were diverse, but most of them could not rely on the family wage system then celebrated in popular culture and public policy. Based on the idea of the male breadwinner as sole provider for dependent wife and children, that system emerged as a compromise between social groups with different interests: white male wage earners, their employers, middle-class reformers (women as well as men), and public officials. Justifying their actions with the notion that men were the *real* family earners, employers paid women inferior wages, and social welfare policies discriminated against them. Yet a large proportion of Americans lacked access to the family wage, among them female household heads and their children, less-skilled workers, and most black, Latino, and Asian American families. Women from these groups became active as never before in the postwar years. Unable to rely on men's incomes and benefiting little from the acclaimed affluence of the era, many looked to labor unions to improve their lives.

Although weakened by the Red Scare, the industrial unions that had surged in the 1930s and 1940s remained a significant force for social justice in the 1950s and 1960s. They created an arena in which many working-class women—white, black, and Latina—began working for gender equality. One example is the powerful United Auto Workers Union (UAW) that, under pressure from the women members who flooded its ranks during the war, set up a Women's Bureau in 1944. UAW women used the union's democratic ideology to bargain for women's needs with employers and to combat the union's internal sexism (see Document 3). "If there had not been a few people like us doing the kinds of things that we have done," the UAW activist Dorothy Haener pointed out in the 1970s, "much of what we have seen happen in the women's movement might well not have happened."[2]

The UAW was the largest union to host such female activism, but other women also used the labor movement as a source of power for gender justice. The left-wing United Electrical Workers (UE) fought for principles that would be considered radical even today, such as differential pay increases for women to close the gender wage gap. It was while working as a labor journalist for the UE in the 1940s that Betty Friedan—who later wrote the clarion call for gender equity, *The Feminine Mystique*—first glimpsed feminism in action. For two decades leading up to the new mass women's movement, union women worked for core feminist demands such as pay equity and employer and government policies to reduce the burden of the "double day" on working mothers. These labor feminists, the historian Dorothy Sue Cobble concludes, "articulated a particular variant of feminism that put the needs of working-class women at its core and . . . championed the labor movement as the principle vehicle through which the lives of the majority of women could be bettered."[3]

CIVIL RIGHTS ORGANIZING OFFERS A WAY FORWARD

By the time President-elect John F. Kennedy urged Americans to "ask what you can do for your country" in his 1961 inaugural address, many women across the country had already answered that question with activism of many kinds. Their organizing built on social and cultural changes that had been accumulating momentum over decades. More and more young Americans—both girls and boys—sought higher education, fulfilling the economy's need for more skilled white-collar workers and their parents' hopes for better futures for their children. Americans also continued their long flight from the countryside to cities and suburbs, whose concentrated populations would make the work of organizers easier. With the United States now the powerhouse of the postwar world economy, millions of Americans were freed from the quest for day-to-day survival to dream larger dreams about what they wanted from life. Still, for the vast majority, utopian hopes remained fixed on private life—until the black civil rights movement returned America's gaze to the public world and its promise.

Nothing so paved the way for a new era of activism for gender equity as the movement for racial equality. Indeed, by far the most consequential women's activism of the late 1950s was in civil rights, as it again became a mass movement, most visibly in the South. While the nation's media focused on male spokespersons such as A. Philip Randolph and the young Reverend Martin Luther King Jr., what made its impact on the nation so powerful were not speeches but committed action by hundreds and thousands of ordinary people who pushed their leaders to lead. And at the grassroots, black women predominated as advocates and organizers for freedom. Taking incredible risks, they often pulled their wider family, church, and community networks into activity.

Within the movement, some black women claimed the ideals of freedom and justice for their gender by challenging male leaders. Anna Arnold Hedgeman protested the absence of women speakers in the plans for the 1963 March on Washington for Jobs and Freedom, commenting that the lack of recognition was shameful "in light of the role of the Negro women in the struggle for freedom and especially in light of the extra burdens they have carried." "Human rights and human dignity are indivisible," the African American attorney and civil rights activist Pauli Murray explained. She criticized a male leader who agreed to speak before the National Press Club, which at that time denied women membership, saying, "Discrimination solely because of sex is just as morally wrong as discrimination because of race."[4]

Black women who demanded fair treatment gained confidence from their history of working outside the home and struggling to ensure the survival of their families. Because job segregation denied nearly all their households the benefits of the family wage, black women innovated, combining employment, child rearing, and homemaking in ways that whites would later emulate. During the postwar years, they earned college and graduate degrees and built professional careers at higher rates than either black men or white women. Those who achieved success often maintained an ethic of community service. Black churches fostered such consciousness, and church participation trained many women in organizing and leadership. At all class levels, women's contributions earned them authority in their communities, which sometimes translated into a willingness to challenge men in ways few white women dared to do. In Mississippi, where involvement meant risking everything, even life itself, organizer Ruby Hurley sometimes recruited by asking a black man if he was "afraid to join the NAACP."[5] Such grassroots activism ultimately transformed national politics as some of the intimidation created by the Red Scare subsided.

The new climate emboldened lesbians and gay men to seek recognition as another "minority" facing unfair discrimination. They built not only on the cultural opening created by civil rights organizing but also on the Fourteenth Amendment's guarantee of equal protection and due process. In 1955, eight San Francisco women formed a new organization called the Daughters of Bilitis (DOB). Seeking to overcome socially imposed isolation and shame over their sexual orientation, they sought to educate the public, break down prejudice, fight censorship, and promote equitable treatment of homosexuals (see Document 4).

Such activism took great courage at a time when it was illegal for women to wear men's clothing, much less have sex with another woman. Every state in the country had criminal "sodomy" laws that outlawed any sexual relations other than heterosexual intercourse. Oral sex even among married couples could lead to a fourteen-year jail term in California, and a teacher suspected of being a lesbian could permanently lose her license. Facing tremendous prejudice and the prospect of criminal prosecution, lesbians had to conceal their identities for survival. DOB founders Del Martin and Phyllis Lyon recalled how San Francisco lesbians hesitated to share identifying information at meetings. They took care not to acknowledge one another on the street, sharing the ethic that "you don't blow anybody's cover." In the very fact of joining together as women to build self-esteem and political confidence, they were also taking a feminist stand. They had concluded that the "homophile" movement, launched five years earlier and led by gay men, was inadequate to advance the concerns of "gay girls," as they called themselves.[6]

As civil rights organizing made advocating social justice a legitimate cause, some women activists pressured President Kennedy to establish the President's Commission on the Status of Women (PCSW) in 1961. Chaired by Eleanor Roosevelt, the commission brought together male and female scholars, public officials, and leaders from a broad spectrum of organizations that had worked to advance gender equity since World War II. The PCSW issued a major report in October 1963 called *American Women* (see Document 7). Outlining an agenda for reform, the report became a best seller. More cautious than CAW's 1946 program, it nonetheless exposed and denounced sex discrimination and affirmed women's right to paid employment. It called for pay equity, child care, paid maternity leave, and other reforms to create substantive equality between men and women. Earlier in 1963, the women's network had won an important victory in the Equal Pay Act, which made it illegal for employers to pay different rates for the same work. The cooperation of women from the ranks of social reform, labor, and civil rights across lines of class, race, region, and religion created an infrastructure for a broad women's movement in the new governors' commissions on the status of women, which operated in every state by 1967.

Also in 1963, Betty Friedan's book *The Feminine Mystique* made visible and urgent what Friedan called "the problem that has no name": the unsettling anxiety felt by growing numbers of middle-class women yearning for a greater purpose in life than ensuring their own nuclear family's well-being. Touching a raw nerve, her work articulated with great poignancy and wit what so many were experiencing. When the mainstream women's magazine *Redbook* asked readers in 1960, "Why do young mothers feel trapped?" it received 24,000 letters.[7] After Friedan's book put a label on the problem, thousands of women who had struggled privately with all kinds of gender-related unhappiness suddenly felt connected to others.

Prior to the 1960s, Friedan straddled three worlds—activism, media, and domesticity—in ways that helped launch a feminist movement. A journalist with a degree from Smith College, Friedan had worked for one of the most progressive unions of the postwar era: the United Electrical Workers. She promoted the UE's message that supporting gender equality would produce a stronger union and a better country. Yet like so many of her war-weary contemporaries, Friedan was anxious to make a home and build a family, and she was very familiar with the world of the suburbs, as well.

In the years of cultural backlash associated with the Red Scare, it was dangerous to talk about gender justice apart from family interests, yet women's lives had been changing in ways that belied the prescriptive ideology of domesticity. Even though women now made up an unprecedented share of students earning college and postgraduate degrees, few employers showed interest in hiring them for any jobs other than low-wage clerical or service work. Still, the numbers of women in the workforce were expanding rapidly, especially among older women. By 1960, three times as many married women were in the workforce as in 1940. The experts claimed with certainty that a "woman's place" was in the home, but experience made women doubt this concept. Taking their cue from black civil rights activists, many working women appropriated the rhetoric of the cold war when they complained that discrimination against women violated America's stated commitment to a free world.

Meanwhile, some of the old penalties for female independence lost their once-potent deterrent effect. The birth control pill was released in 1960, and within a year, a million women were taking it. By 1970, six in every ten adult women exercised some form of birth control. With unwanted pregnancy no longer such a risk, single women were freer to enjoy sex and experiment in ways that would have been unthinkable for their grandmothers. In their generation, a "shotgun wedding" to remedy an out-of-wedlock pregnancy had caused public shame, and illegal abortions carried the risk of death. As love and intimacy became prized as the basis for relationships, the idea of stigmatizing children born to unmarried mothers as "illegitimate," even ostracizing them as "bastards," struck more and more people as inappropriate in a democracy. Divorce, too, was becoming more common and accepted. Life expectancy was increasing such that by 1970, a woman faced the prospect of thirty years after her last child left home. "It is commonly asserted that feminism is responsible for a weakening of the family," as a pioneer scholar of women's history explains, "when in fact it is the case that the demands raised by feminism are answers to the problems posed by an already changed family and life cycle."[8]

Surging civil rights activism offered an inspiring model for solving social problems through collective action. The lunch counter sit-ins begun by four black college students in Greensboro, North Carolina, in February 1960 galvanized African American young people all across the South. Within a week, sit-ins had spread to fifteen cities in five states, and black and white sympathizers in the North picketed local branches of the lunch counter chains in solidarity. All told, more people took part than had ever participated in any prior civil rights struggle — some 70,000 within a year and a half. Hundreds of southern communities desegregated their public eating facilities within months.

The example of the North Carolina students inspired the formation of the Student Nonviolent Coordinating Committee (SNCC). SNCC generated the most creative and courageous activism of the 1960s in its community organizing and voter registration projects in the Deep South. In its first years, SNCC proved unusually egalitarian in relations between men and women — precisely because it was so committed to democracy and equality. Its activists were guided by the radical democratic philosophy of an older woman, Ella Baker, who helped SNCC get started. She stressed the importance of enabling ordinary men and women to *become* leaders (see Document 5).

The commitment of southern black students inspired northern white students' activism. In the 1962 Port Huron Statement, the newly formed Students for a Democratic Society (SDS) articulated themes that would influence not only a generation of campus activism but also feminism. Calling for "a democracy of authentic participation," SDS organizers founded the Economic Research and Action Project (ERAP), which brought the SNCC organizing model to northern urban communities in hopes of building "an interracial movement of the poor." SDS women found that they excelled as organizers, largely because they listened and learned from the low-income women who were the behind-the-scenes neighborhood leaders. Through their successes, SDS female organizers acquired confidence and political know-how.

Meanwhile, the mounting civil rights struggle turned public opinion against racial discrimination. By 1964, 85 percent of Americans told pollsters they supported equal employment opportunity for blacks and whites, putting heavy pressure on the federal government to act to promote justice. President Lyndon B. Johnson waged a determined and successful battle to get Congress to pass a strong Civil Rights Act that year. In the summer of 1965, the new federal Equal Employment Opportunity Commission started work. Its mission, established in Title VII of the Civil Rights Act, was to open America's workplaces to all citizens on a fair and equal basis.

THE NEW FEMINISM OF THE "SECOND WAVE"

The ban on employment discrimination proved a huge shot in the arm to the large numbers of adult women activists who had quietly continued to seek gender equity even after the cold war subdued more radical organizing. They were galvanized to new boldness by the EEOC's refusal to recognize sex discrimination as a serious problem. Watching these events unfold, the black trade unionist Dollie Robinson suggested that supporters of gender justice needed an "NAACP for women."[9] Pauli Murray, who first coined the phrase "Jane Crow" in the 1940s to describe the system that held women down, gave a speech in the fall of 1965 announcing that Title VII would do nothing for women unless they organized. Newspaper reports of the speech led Betty Friedan to seek out Murray, who then introduced Friedan to the women of the PCSW network. A year later, in 1966, this core group formed a new "civil rights organization," the National Organization for Women (NOW; see Figure 1). Very few of the women who initially formed NOW were newcomers to political action. Contrary to the notion that they were stereotypical East Coast suburbanites, the vast majority of the founders were from the Midwest, where most had been active in social reform for years. For example, Caroline Davis

"Hire him. He's got great legs."

If women thought this way about men they would be awfully silly.

When men think this way about women they're silly, too.

Women should be judged for a job by whether or not they can do it.

In a world where women are doctors, lawyers, judges, brokers, economists, scientists, political candidates, professors and company presidents, any other viewpoint is ridiculous.

Think of it this way. When we need all the help we can get, why waste half the brains around?

Womanpower. It's much too good to waste.

This advertisement prepared for Ms. magazine by volunteers through deGarmo, Inc. for the National Organization for Women.

Figure 1. *"Hire Him, He's Got Great Legs," 1971*
In the early 1970s, the National Organization for Women (NOW) worked with volunteer advertising professionals to produce a public service ad campaign that used humor to demonstrate the absurdity of sexist thinking. The ads appeared in print and broadcast media across the country and contributed to changing ideas about gender and women's capacities.

Courtesy of Legal Momentum (formerly NOW Legal Defense and Education Fund).

and Dorothy Haener persuaded their union, the UAW, to supply crucial seed money and clerical support to launch NOW.

At first, NOW focused on employment equity but made clear that its interests extended to maternity leave and child care; equal education; a woman's right to control her own fertility; and passage of the Equal Rights Amendment (ERA) to signify public recognition that women were entitled to full citizenship (see Document 9). Together, these demands promised to level the playing field between the sexes by providing support for women to deal with the family responsibilities that weighed on them so heavily and put them at a disadvantage in public life. NOW soon became the largest feminist organization in the United States; its membership grew from fourteen chapters in 1967 with 1,000 members to more than 700 chapters with 40,000 members by 1974.

The Civil Rights Act proved vital to advancing the new movement, not simply because it sparked NOW but also because it enabled a realignment of women's politics (see Document 8). When women were finally promised an end to sex discrimination on the job, the bitter forty-year split over the ERA became moot. The tension between middle-class white feminists, who would benefit the most from ending sex segregation, and working-class women, who feared the ERA might threaten legal protections for working women, finally abated. Indeed, Title VII altered the terrain of women's and progressive politics fundamentally. It enabled new cross-class alliances among women, coalitions between feminists and the labor and civil rights movements, and novel collaborations linking older social reform–minded women with younger women seeking new personal freedoms and more radical social change.

Younger women, typically recent college graduates, developed a distinctive current of the emerging mass movement: women's liberation. From their participation in the black freedom movement, the campus-based New Left, and antiwar activism, young women gained ideas and strategies, experience in organizing, role models of female strength, and networks of communication with which to spread ideas for change. Like the abolitionist women before them, these young women became more aware of *sexism* (a word they coined), and their political experience gave them the confidence to challenge it more vocally by the mid-sixties.[10] In response to the escalating war in Vietnam and continuing racial injustice at home, these activists became more radical. They challenged what they called "the system" of capitalism and imperialism, not just particular injustices.

One ironic result of that radicalization was that both SNCC and SDS became less hospitable to women, particularly white women. Because the Red Scare had devastated the American left, most young radicals looked abroad for models, especially to the revolutionary guerrilla struggles in Asia, Africa, and Latin America. Young men in particular equated radical change with military struggle and a kind of masculine bravado that diminished women in all but the most conventional roles. The changes in SNCC and SDS made the movements to which young white women had formerly devoted their energies less attractive. Becoming more aware of women's issues, some budding feminists stayed on to fight from within mixed-sex movements, whereas others chose to strike out on their own. Whatever their differences, women's liberation members aimed to change everyday life and culture in the process of changing the world and linked sexism to class injustice, racism, and colonialism. On both fronts, they considered NOW too "liberal" (as opposed to radical) and criticized it for working within "the system."

Young women focused new critical attention on intimate relationships. They were at the prime age for refashioning personal identity, at a time when the New Left and the youth "counterculture" both strived for personal "authenticity" and cultural transformation. Twice as many women engaged in sexual intercourse before marriage in the 1960s as in the 1950s. They were agents, alongside their male partners, of a newly expressive, pleasure-seeking, nonprocreative sexuality that many observers depicted as a "sexual revolution." But women soon learned that this was a confusing revolution. For example, with effective birth control available, women found it harder to say no to intercourse even when they did not want it. Thus, although women had more freedom to be sexual, men were defining what constituted "liberation."

To explore their issues, women's liberationists developed a process called "consciousness raising" (C-R) that they used to explore fresh questions about gender and power in everyday life (see Document 10). Sharing their experiences and feelings with other women in an atmosphere of mutual support, participants realized that they faced societywide problems that were rooted in power relationships and could be changed through collective action. Adopting the slogan "The personal is political" to convey this understanding, C-R groups analyzed a wide range of issues. Through discussions, they learned that fear of pregnancy undermined women's sexual pleasure, as the specters of an unwanted child or an unsafe abortion hampered love making (see Document 11). They learned that many of them faked orgasms. And women reported a surprising frequency of what would later be called "date rape" or "acquaintance rape."

Activists soon realized that no area of life was free of sexism. Turning to housework, they began to question why women were expected to do all of it, and they shared stories of strategies men used to get out of doing their fair share (see Document 17). At their workplaces, they saw how job segregation was routine, as was the assumption that a woman in an office should act as a surrogate wife to male coworkers by making coffee and providing personal services (see Document 29). When they compared their experiences in school, women agreed that male teachers seldom took them as seriously as male students (see Document 13). The media treated women as mindless sex objects to sell otherwise unappealing products. Worst of all, women had internalized these denigrating norms through years of conditioning and fear of reprisal for defying them. The discussions led to the realization that to achieve even simple fairness, women had to transform American culture and institutions.

Women's liberation activists developed what they called "sexual politics" or "personal politics" to challenge male domination in both intimate relations and the wider world. Some of the themes of the new sexual politics were not entirely new. In earlier decades, women, both black and white, had exposed the sexual double standard and the familial division of labor in biting satires (see Document 2). Yet the cold war climate had driven such criticism underground, so these young women believed they were discovering entirely new territory.

As these two currents of explicit feminism were developing, poor women began organizing as never before, with black mothers who had been influenced by civil rights in the lead. Proclaiming that "welfare is a right" and not some shameful charity for which they should be humbly grateful, recipients of Aid to Families with Dependent Children moved their needs to the center of national discussion in the 1960s. In 1966, a number of local groups joined together to form the National Welfare Rights Organization (NWRO), a movement that at its peak involved more than 20,000 women. NWRO waged successful campaigns to obtain grants for poor mothers for items such as school clothes for their children and household equipment. But just as important, these women gained more respectful treatment as citizens by winning the right to due process and fair hearings before termination of any benefit to which they were entitled. They also came close to winning a guaranteed annual income base for all Americans. Welfare rights activists did not begin as feminists, but they were highly gender-conscious in their pursuit of respect and compensation for the vital work of raising children, and they became feminists over time (see Document 22).

Latina farmworkers also organized on the basis of maternal identities shaped by class and race. In the West and Southwest, tens of thousands of Mexican Americans worked in the fields in grueling conditions for low pay and few, if any, benefits, due to the exclusion of agricultural workers from the labor legislation of the New Deal. Children worked alongside their parents; many suffered from malnutrition and occupational ailments and died young. Women agonized over the fate of their children but could do little to protect them because their households so desperately needed the income. In 1962, a new labor association led by César Chávez and Dolores Huerta began to organize these communities. From the beginning, the United Farm Workers sought to involve women. "The women have to be involved," Chávez and Huerta told farmworker families. "If you can take the women out into the fields, you can certainly take them to meetings." Jessie Lopez de la Cruz, who had been working since she was a child, jumped at the chance to rectify these injustices. "It was very hard being a woman organizer," she recalled later, because many farmworkers "were raised with the old customs in Mexico" that "the husband rules" and "the wife obeys"—ideas they brought to the organization (see Document 21). But female union members persevered and played especially vital roles in strikes that gradually won them recognition.[11]

CHANGING CULTURE AND POLICY

In the summer of 1970, women old and young of varied backgrounds came together in a broad coalition for the first mass demonstration of second-wave feminism, the Women's Strike for Equality, to commemorate the fiftieth anniversary of the Nineteenth Amendment. Virtually every feminist group across the spectrum mobilized for the strike. "Don't iron while the strike is hot," some rally posters punned. On August 26, 1970, tens of thousands marched in cities across the country, calling for three central demands: equal opportunity for women in employment and education, the right to abortion, and the right to child care.

Immediately after the event, the veteran radical civil rights activist and black attorney Eleanor Holmes Norton convened the first major feminist public hearing of the era on "Women's Role in Contemporary Society." Then head of the New York City Commission on Human

Rights, Norton brought together representatives from dozens of organizations and institutions to reveal the range and depth of the problems women experienced and to propose solutions. She used the hearings to urge the new feminist activists toward broad-based coalitions that would advance the interests of all women and of disadvantaged men, thus creating majority backing for substantive reforms. While praising the movement for "indispensable and brilliant" consciousness raising, Norton urged an "organized, rather than hit-and-miss, strategy for change."[12]

Through the work of strategic thinkers such as Norton, the new feminism reached and energized a broad array of venerable women's organizations. Some, like the American Association of University Women (AAUW), the League of Women Voters, and the YWCA, had large memberships and significant resources. All embarked on action agendas that used the power of their numbers and their organizational experience to strengthen the movement. The older women who for decades had organized without recognition or fanfare thus proved critical in enabling feminists to achieve so much so quickly. NOW and the young women's liberationists were not working alone; they had these organizations with much larger memberships and long-standing credibility backing up their push for change.

Working on so many fronts, the women's movement acquired additional allies with regularity, including some very committed men. The older women of NOW, more experienced in coalition building and more committed to majoritarian politics, welcomed men as members and often worked with them in electoral politics. That paid off when men who worked for the EEOC and had a lot to offer to gender equity because of their experience became committed allies. Other progressive men, such as Winn Newman, worked with women in nonfeminist organizations to produce change. As chief legal counsel for the International Union of Electrical Workers (IUE) after 1972, Newman allied with female union members and worked for gender equity with aggressive policies to uproot discrimination.

Women's liberationists, in contrast, tended to advocate all-women's organizations. Some did so from a philosophical commitment to "autonomy" and "sisterhood" that was modeled on the turn to separatism among Black Power activists. Others did so from a practical standpoint, impatient with the way sexism among male activists stifled women's creativity and held back action for progress. Still, some young men supported the movement's goals in an auxiliary capacity at a respectful distance (see Document 15).

INTRODUCTION **21**

The spreading commitment to self-determination for women emboldened lesbians to demand that homophobia be recognized as a women's
issue, a problem analogous to racism and sexism in how it sustained
injustice. They became especially vocal in the wake of the Stonewall
rebellion of 1969, when New York gays fought back against police
repression in a clash that spurred a "gay liberation" movement. Invig-
orated by mass struggle, lesbians and gay men in growing numbers
came "out of the closet" to show that they were "everywhere" and "out
and proud," as some new slogans put it. They organized with newfound
confidence, launching dozens of gay newspapers, organizations, and
direct actions. In 1973, gay activists scored a huge victory when the
American Psychiatric Association recognized the "normality" of homosexuality and no longer defined it as a disorder that needed treatment.

Lesbians, however, encountered resistance from those they looked
to as allies. The gay liberation movement at first seemed congenial to
women but, like other institutions of the time, was soon dominated by
men. Moreover, it seemed that gay men's version of sexual liberation
was an extreme form of all that feminists found troubling in heterosexual male sexuality, especially casual sex with multiple partners
with little interest in them as people. As lesbians turned away from
gay men and toward their feminist "sisters," they found heterosexual
feminists hardly immune from the homophobia that was pervasive in
American society. Most notoriously, Betty Friedan warned in 1970 of a
"lavender menace" to NOW and to feminism. Many others voiced
their biases just as openly and tried to silence lesbians by claiming
that their visibility provided ammunition to antifeminists.

Some lesbians responded by arguing that lesbians, as totally
"women-identified women," were the only *real* feminists. They accused
heterosexual women of "collaborating" with the enemy, meaning men
(see Document 20). In the 1970s, they vocally challenged homophobia
and energetically advanced their vision (see Figure 2). Fierce, sometimes debilitating, conflicts split more than a few organizations.

Still, lesbian feminists brought profound analytical insights to the
women's movement. Because they derived no benefits from the old
system of gender hierarchy, they were in a better position to identify
and act on its ugly underpinnings. And whereas fear of male disap-
proval might silence heterosexual women, lesbian feminists were free
of such fear. They spoke plainly about the issues as they saw them,
and they challenged "straight" women. Why did women socialize with
men who diminished their dignity and humanity? What did this say
about a woman's self-respect? They pointed out how homophobia

Figure 2. *"Sexual Freedom Means All of Us,"* 1975

The signs at this June 1975 Gay Pride march in New York City suggest the divisions that homophobia was causing in the women's movement. Emboldened by feminism and the gay liberation movement, lesbians became increasingly visible and vocal, playing leading roles in both causes.

entrenched women's and men's gender roles and thus constrained individual autonomy while reinforcing gender hierarchy. Lesbians also taught feminists that sexuality is socially constructed: what people desire and do sexually, and with whom and how, is shaped not only by nature but also by culture—and above all by relations of power in their society.

Because lesbians had the most to gain from a better world for women, they contributed disproportionately to the movement. They were at the forefront of the struggle against violence against women, for example. In 1970 and 1971, feminists labeled rape as a form of terrorism that kept women subordinate by frightening them and restricting their mobility (see Document 19). Antirape activists exposed how the penal system enforced male power by always blaming the rape victim. Women's liberation activists, lesbians among them, not only offered a new understanding of rape but also devised innovative means to address it. They established rape crisis centers and hotlines to aid victims and work for change, taught self-defense to women, and educated the public and law enforcement officials on how to respond to and reduce sexual violence. Feminists also tackled the problems of date rape and marital rape, which was legal in most of the country in the 1970s.

These efforts led to new awareness of domestic violence, long protected by the legal doctrine of home privacy (see Document 28). As late as 1976, 90 percent of U.S. police departments would not routinely arrest perpetrators of domestic abuse. Feminists learned that full-time homemakers were particularly susceptible due to their economic dependence on their husbands. Activists opened shelters as places of refuge for battered women, where they could also obtain legal advice, child care, counseling, and help in locating housing and employment. Along with such collective self-help projects, feminists developed other institutions in the 1970s such as women's bookstores, coffeehouses, athletic teams, publishers, and music festivals.

The vital contributions that lesbians made to developing feminism and women's culture began to undermine the legitimacy of homophobia. As straight activists came to appreciate their lesbian sisters' arguments and saw for themselves how some men used lesbian-baiting to stifle female self-assertion, many changed their thinking. A year after Friedan's "lavender menace" comment, for example, NOW passed a resolution recognizing that what made lesbians seem so threatening to a sexist culture was their independence of men. NOW also stated that lesbian rights were integral to sexual self-determination for all women. Growing numbers were coming to understand how women, especially the young women most susceptible to peer pressure, could be intimidated from standing up for themselves by suggestions that feminists were "man-hating lesbians." As Gloria Steinem, a leading heterosexual feminist often featured in the news, put it: "As long as we fear the word 'lesbian' we are curtailing our own strength and abandoning our sisters. As long as human sexuality is politically controlled, we will all be losing a basic human freedom."[13]

In response to the growing women's movement, in the early 1970s, the U.S. Congress passed more legislation for women's rights than ever before or since. In 1972 alone, the House and the Senate passed the ERA and sent it out to the states for ratification. Other legislation provided tax breaks for working parents and approved Title IX of the Higher Education Act to provide for gender equity in education and athletics. Pressure from the full array of women's organizations had, meanwhile, convinced the EEOC to enforce laws against sex discrimination in employment and include women in affirmative action programs designed to ensure equal hiring and promotion opportunities. Such government action opened better jobs at all levels to women and created more fairness in promotions, pay, and benefits.

Another victory of the early 1970s was the decriminalization of abortion. Prior to 1973, approximately 10,000 American women died each year from botched illegal abortions; nearly half were poor women of color. Because of this danger, doctors had pushed for abortion law repeal beginning in the early 1960s. By 1969, a nationwide poll found that 64 percent of Americans believed that "the decision on abortion should be a private one." Feminists further argued that women could not be free or equal if they lacked the ability to determine whether and when they had children. If a woman could not control her own body, she would be powerless in other arenas. She had the moral authority to decide a question so fundamental to her life.

Making the elimination of state and federal criminal abortion laws their goal, activists fought for a woman's legal access to safe abortions. Defying convention, they even spoke publicly about personal experiences of unwanted pregnancy and humiliating, even life-threatening, illicit abortions (see Document 11). They also demonstrated at medical conventions, stormed public hearings, and held sit-ins at hospitals. Some women's liberationists defied the laws by organizing an underground abortion service in Chicago in 1969. Given the code name "Jane," the service provided safe, high-quality procedures for women who might otherwise turn to dangerous back-alley abortions. Jane arranged for over 11,000 abortions, with a safety record that rivaled private clinics.

This context of profound social change and broad political opposition to the existing laws helps explain why the Supreme Court ruled in *Roe v. Wade* in 1973 that the right to privacy protected a woman's right to choose abortion. By then, seventeen states had liberalized their abortion statutes. Earlier, in its *Griswold v. Connecticut* decision of 1965, the high court had established that the right to privacy protected birth control information hitherto illegal under many states' obscenity laws. With access to contraception and safe abortions, more women could work, pursue advanced education, and be sexually active if they so chose without the risk of unwanted pregnancy.

The emerging women's health movement further transformed women's relationships with their bodies. Building on the combined insights of feminism and the radicalism of the era, it identified how sexism in the medical profession and a for-profit health care delivery system combined to produce terrible results for women, among them frequent radical surgeries such as hysterectomies, rather than holistic guidance toward healthy living (see Document 18). Arising from informal discussions at a Boston women's liberation conference in 1969, by 1973 the women's health movement included over twelve hundred groups. One of the galvanizing forces was a popular and accessible self-help guide to women's health, published by the Boston Women's Health Collective, a group of twelve women who researched various aspects of women's physiology, in 1970. The first newsprint issue sold 250,000 copies within three years. The group then contracted with a major commercial publisher, demanding steep discounts for nonprofit health organizations and signing over all royalties to the women's health movement. *Our Bodies, Ourselves* ultimately sold millions of copies in twenty languages. It modeled the best of the new movement in its attention to women's diversity, and also connected body and mind and united self-care with commitment to building community. Above all, it provided women with the knowledge they needed to exert more control over their lives.

The emerging women's health movement tackled a wide range of reproductive policy issues. Challenging medical paternalism, feminists made doctors and hospitals more accountable to patients. One early campaign concerned the safety of birth control pills that contained high dosages of hormones and had serious side effects such as blood clots, diabetes, and strokes. Pharmaceutical companies also conducted experiments on vulnerable poor women to test products they planned to market to wealthier women. By 1977, feminists had won both warning labels and the development of lower-dosage birth control pills. Another campaign focused on the widely used intra-uterine device (IUD), a birth control device that was surgically inserted into the uterus. Although many women suffered from perforated uteruses and other complications, male doctors continued to promote it on the grounds that it did not interfere with men's pleasure during intercourse.

The most politically important health care struggle was the one waged against the involuntary sterilization of poor women, especially Latinas, African Americans, and Native Americans, often as a condition for receiving public assistance (see Figure 3). In New York, Puerto Rican liberation activists first drew attention to the high levels of sterilization of Puerto Rican women. Led by feminists within the Young Lords Party, they distinguished between the right of women to choose abortion or sterilization, and the enforcement of such procedures on them for social control purposes (see Document 16). Black feminists in the early 1970s also criticized sterilization abuse targeting poor women as they taught white feminists about the need for a reproductive politics that went beyond abortion rights.

In 1977, New York activists organized the Committee for Abortion Rights and Against Sterilization Abuse (CARASA), which included Dr. Helen Rodriguez-Trias, an early medical whistle-blower and opponent of sterilization abuse, and veteran socialist feminists (see Documents 23 and 30). Participants criticized the slogan of "choice" used by liberal feminists and mainstream abortion rights organizations for failing to capture the situation of women whose decisions were constrained by poverty and poor health care. CARASA educated the public about how coercive sterilization combined racism, sexism, and class discrimination to deny women autonomy over their own reproduction. The group also demanded that hospitals stop performing it. "Reproductive freedom," as the pamphlet *Women under Attack* explained, "means the freedom to have as well as not to have children. Policies that restrict [some] women's right to have and raise children —through forced sterilization or denial of adequate welfare benefits— are directly related to policies that compel [other] women to have children, on the view that this is their primary human function."[14]

Differences in perspective and clashes over goals and strategy became evident as more voices joined the discussion about gender. Most activists who embraced the label "feminist" in the 1960s were white women from middle-class backgrounds. Self-styled "radical

Figure 3. *"Sterilization Abuse Is a Crime against the People," 1973*
Prompted by Puerto Rican activists, black and white socialist feminists organized against the involuntary sterilization of poor women in the 1970s. Criticizing liberal feminists for focusing too narrowly on abortion rights, they developed a politics of "reproductive rights" that also included freedom from sterilization abuse and the positive right of women to bear children they desired and have healthy and safe conditions in which to rear them.

feminists," in particular, constituted the whitest wing of the women's movement. Proclaiming gender the key determinant in life, they presumed to speak for all women, imagining that their own distinctive experience of womanhood denoted a "universal sisterhood." They issued manifestos on the shared needs of all women without consulting women unlike themselves. And they urged women to put gender first, ahead of class or race, arguing that those who failed to do so were selling out (see Document 20).

Women of color and many working-class women angrily disputed such analysis. Black women, including Pauli Murray and Eleanor Holmes Norton, had played key roles in setting the agenda of the feminist movement, but they insisted on the irreducible importance of racism and the need for solidarity with other people who were fighting oppression. Most black women viewed the young white feminists' talk of radical sisterhood as more rhetoric than substance. They pointed to the white women's limited understanding of racial injustice as emblematic of an underlying particularism, even blindness, to the situation of oppressed people who were situated differently. Soon other women of color were criticizing the way many white feminists were construing their goals (see Documents 21, 26, 30, 32, and 36). No one defined the challenge better than Barbara Smith, who announced in 1979, "Feminism is the political theory and practice to free all women: women of color, working-class women, poor women, physically challenged women, lesbians, old women—as well as white economically privileged heterosexual women. Anything less than this is not feminism, but merely female self-aggrandizement."[15]

Above all, most black and Latina women activists rejected the separatism of the "radical feminists." They felt a pressing need for solidarity with the men with whom they shared experiences of racism and felt little affinity with the white feminists who now called them "sisters." As women of color focused more on gender justice, they typically did so within their own mixed-sex organizations that were working for racial justice or in groups with other women of color. In 1972, the first national conference of Mexican American women met in Houston, Texas, and, after vigorous discussion, passed resolutions specific to their situation and needs (see Document 21). Eleanor Holmes Norton joined with other black women to found the National Black Feminist Organization in 1973; within a year, it had grown to 2,000 members in ten cities (see Document 26). Similarly, working-class women by and large also rejected separatism and preferred to work through their unions or community groups in the belief that cooperation with men was the best strategy for the changes they wanted to achieve (see Document 25). Nearly all such activists stressed that women could not achieve equality apart from wider social transformation.

Working-class women of varied backgrounds also organized for gender justice in their own venues. Feminists in the labor movement assembled in Chicago in 1974 to create the Coalition of Labor Union Women (CLUW). In 1975, activists in Brooklyn, New York, founded the National Congress of Neighborhood Women to be a unifying voice for poor and working-class women of varied backgrounds, many of them Italian American. They opened a shelter for battered women, established a community college program that educated organizers, worked on tenants' rights with black-led groups, and provided job

Figure 4. *"Minority Women Unite for Equal Rights, Day Care, Jobs, Abortion," 1977*

Participating in an International Women's Day event in 1977, these activists highlighted the broad range of issues for which women of color organized. Black feminists in particular insisted on the need to fight racism and tackle poverty. They exposed the practical and ideological connections among sexism, racism, class hierarchy, and homophobia.

© Freda Leinwand 1977.

training and placement for unemployed women. By the time of the Houston conference in 1977, virtually every feminist identity or goal had an organization (see Figure 4).

As more communities added their voices to the public debate on women and gender, feminists began to understand difference as a potential source of strength. The pitched conflicts over racism, homophobia, and class bias, painful as they were, taught at least some participants important lessons. Pushed to recognize their own biases and prodded to live up to their beliefs in equality and democracy, many feminists developed a commitment to diversity that equipped them for better organizing than their male contemporaries. Some white, middle-class women became deeply committed to economic and racial justice (see Document 34). Church Women United, for example, developed a faith-anchored feminism that sought universal equality and justice and worked for it in practical ways, initiating such projects as Women in Community Service (WICS) to aid women and children who were living in poverty. The League of Women Voters devoted extensive energy and resources to the cause of welfare rights, and in 1970, the YWCA, led by Dorothy Height, formerly president of the National Council of Negro Women, made "the elimination of racism" its "one imperative."[16]

The variety of perspectives was proof that one type of "feminism" could never prove capacious enough for all women. The contrasting and evolving ways that women experienced gender meant that many "feminisms" would exist. Advocates did not have to agree on one set of ideas or demands to be part of the same historical process. In 1981, SNCC veteran Bernice Johnson Reagon summarized this rising awareness with a challenge: "There is nowhere you can go and only be with people who are like you." Coalition was the only way forward. "The reason we are stumbling is that we are at the point where in order to take the next step we've got to do it with some folk we don't care too much about." Personal comfort was less important than taking the struggle to the next stage, because no single group could achieve its goals in isolation from others now. "Stretch your perimeter," Reagon advised. "If you feel the strain, you may be doing some good work." Through this stretching process, participants learned to appreciate diversity, and they spread that newfound appreciation throughout the wider culture.

Feminists stretched across boundaries of ideology as well as experience. Indeed, what stands out most with a quarter-century of hindsight is the way the different elements of the movement cross-pollinated. As some activists concentrated on cultural innovation and others on legal reform and institutional change, each abetted the other in advancing real and important improvements. The older women, long called "liberal feminists" because of their work "through the system" for changes in law and public policy, believed substantive reform such as publicly supported quality child care was vital. Because most of them were mothers themselves, they understood the limits of gender-blind formal equality. Just *saying* that discrimination should end did not help the women who were struggling to combine paid employment, child raising, and housework. On the other side, the younger women who styled themselves "radical feminists" knew that cultural change and alternative institutions alone would not solve such problems as rape, domestic violence, and homophobia. They also had to change the way the legal system worked. In large parts of the country, away from media magnets like New York City and Washington, D.C., the differences between political currents in the movement were less pronounced or even nonexistent. In the communities inhabited by most feminists, the shared commitment to a better world for women loomed larger than ideological disputes, although they were still concerned with various controversies.[17] All vibrant social movements have diverse wings, based partly on different social networks and partly on politics, and sometimes they clash furiously, as was the case with abolition, organized labor, and civil rights. In the women's movement, people concentrated on what they cared about most or were the best at, tackling manageable pieces of the larger project in ways that ultimately transformed the whole society.

As many types of feminists educated one another, the range of "women's issues" expanded. The overwhelmingly female welfare rights movement thus drew attention to measurable realities that some feminist journalists and social scientists called the "feminization of poverty" (see Document 22). Women headed the majority of poor households, and the majority of female-headed households *were* poor, not only in the United States but also worldwide. Female poverty, they demonstrated, was partly rooted in a sexual division of labor, often working in conjunction with a racial division of labor, that both segregates women into lower-paying jobs and gives them sole responsibility for child rearing and housework. Many fathers did not financially support their children after divorce, which happened to one out of every two marriages (see Figure 5). To help women free themselves from poverty, some feminists undertook an ambitious effort to open skilled construction trades jobs to women, jobs that typically paid more than twice as much as women with limited education could earn in so-called women's jobs. The effort to help women obtain well-paid work occurred in all parts of the country with government job-training funds. In 1978, as a result of a lawsuit filed by feminists, President Jimmy Carter announced affirmative action goals and timetables for women in construction jobs.

The biggest advances came in areas where varied groups, not only feminists, had long been pushing for change and where majorities agreed on goals. The women's movement thus achieved its widest diversity of backers and scored its greatest successes in employment. Second-wave feminism was centrally concerned with the needs of women who could not rely on a male-earned family wage. Historically,

these were women of color and white working-class women. Only by the 1960s did a large number of white middle-class women discover that they were vulnerable, too. Their combined push for economic security opened up jobs to women even in the most hostile occupations. It changed the way millions thought about women's and men's capacities and thus altered "common sense" about gender. While opening a new realm of jobs to women, the coalitions built around employment also allowed feminists to make unprecedented headway on such vital matters as maternity leave, workplace sexual harassment, and greater employer and government support for parenting (see Document 29).

THE CONSERVATIVE BACKLASH

Given the scale of the challenge the women's movement posed to long-established power relations and cultural assumptions, some backlash was inevitable. Few feminists were prepared, however, for how deep-rooted and effective it was. The countermovement united long-time conservative organizers with church-based forces at the grass-roots who disapproved of the changes in gender and sexual norms. Just as the feminist surge built on the foundations of earlier decades, so did the antifeminist backlash. Committed to free-market economics, states' rights politics, aggressive anticommunist foreign policy, and social traditionalism, conservative leaders fought New Deal programs and civil rights legislation. In the 1960s, they fought feminism as well as the wider radical democratic upheaval.

The backlash attracted avid grassroots support around the country in 1972, when Phyllis Schlafly, a longtime conservative activist, founded STOP ERA to block passage of the Equal Rights Amendment. By then, most liberals supported the ERA, among them nearly all mainstream

---

(Opposite) **Figure 5.** *"Divorce Insurance for Housewives: Knockout Poverty and Dependency," 1970*
Feminists identified and acted on the plight of "displaced homemakers"— women who devoted themselves to raising their children and working in the home, only to face poverty and neglect after divorce or the death of their husbands. As the women-led welfare rights movement deepened awareness of the ties among gender, race, child rearing, and poverty in America, some feminists organized campaigns to address "the feminization of poverty," the pattern in which women headed the majority of households below the poverty line.
Photo © by Bettye Lane. Reprinted with permission of Donna McAlpine.

women's groups, black civil rights groups, the AFL-CIO, and Congress by over a 10 to 1 margin. Using her newsletter to mobilize opposition, Schlafly warned that feminism would undermine "the rights women already have," and above all, "the right to be a housewife."[18] Schlafly appealed to those who were uneasy with the demise of the family wage system and changing gender and sexual mores and fearful for the future. She concentrated on feminism's vulnerabilities, among them a propensity for inflammatory critiques of conventional families (see Document 14), an emphasis on personal freedom that could be construed as individualism heedless of others' needs, and a focus on abuse that could appear to embrace "victimhood" (see Document 24).

Portraying themselves as the defenders of "traditional family values," social conservatives also began to find a new base of popular support in churches that opposed abortion and gender equality. In 1973, the year the Supreme Court ruled in *Roe v. Wade*, the National Council of Catholic Bishops created the National Committee for a Human Life Amendment to lobby for a constitutional amendment that would overturn the Court's decision. Two years later, the bishops issued a pastoral letter entitled *Pastoral Plan for Pro-Life Activities* that contained detailed instructions on how to organize "pro-life" groups in every congressional district, in part to get "pro-choice" politicians out of office. White evangelicals, whose numbers surged in the 1970s to the tens of millions, joined Catholics in the mobilization by the decade's end.

While church-based organizing provided the driving force of the opposition to legal abortion, conservatives also set up secular organizations. In particular, the National Right to Life Committee (NRLC) became the largest anti-abortion coalition, with a claimed 11,000 supporters by the late 1970s. The organizations were usually led by men at the national level, but women made up the bulk of their supporters and activists—80 percent in one national survey. The vast majority were full-time homemakers and regular churchgoers. Over the ensuing years, the right-to-life campaign secured restrictions that cut off access to abortion for growing numbers of women, even while abortion remained legal and technically available. The Hyde Amendment, for example, prohibited the use of federal funds for abortions and so denied the procedure to low-income women who depended on Medicaid. First adopted in 1977, the Hyde Amendment was passed year after year. Impatient, some abortion opponents turned to direct action: by 1985, 80 percent of clinics had experienced picketing and harassment of patients and staff.

Opposition to gay rights emerged as a third focus of the backlash. Like the fight against abortion, it attracted many working-class Christians who were once part of the Democratic New Deal coalition but were also committed to a patriarchal model of family life and church orthodoxy on sexuality. Extremely hostile to homosexuality, conservative movement builders escalated their attack as the gay movement gained ground. After a successful 1977 challenge to a Miami ordinance prohibiting discrimination against gays, they organized more and more ballot challenges to such measures, at least fifty of which have succeeded. Seeing the power such efforts had in encouraging conservative voters to go to the polls, leaders of the Republican right made the fight against gay rights central to their program.

In 1979, the conservative strategists Paul Weyrich and Richard Viguerie urged the Virginia fundamentalist Baptist minister and television evangelist Jerry Falwell to form an organization to counter the authority of liberal religious groups in American life. Falwell founded the Moral Majority, which linked antifeminism and antihomosexual advocacy to long-standing conservative causes: anticommunism, promotion of "free enterprise," hostility to welfare and federally funded human services, and an aggressive foreign policy. "Jesus," Falwell taught his followers, "was not a sissy"[19] (see Document 33). Falwell's Moral Majority was joined by the Religious Roundtable, a network of conservative politicians and ministers. Taken together, these organizations made up what came to be called the New Right, which distinguished itself with its zealous concern over gender and sexual issues and with a populist style that characterized liberals as effete, elite, and far removed from ordinary Americans.

A key shift in the balance of power between feminism and antifeminism was the election of the conservative movement's standard bearer, Ronald Reagan, to the presidency in 1980. With Reagan heading the ticket, the Republican Party reversed forty years of support for the Equal Rights Amendment, while the new president soon blamed working women for high unemployment rates. "Feminism kind of became the focus of everything," recalled a libertarian economist then employed at the Heritage Foundation, a conservative think tank that regularly advised the Reagan administration in the 1980s. "The feminists became this very identifiable target."[20]

Conservative success over the next quarter-century made it difficult for the women's movement to achieve any major new victories. The struggle to hold their endangered ground consumed feminists' energy and resources. This was especially true of NOW, the only remaining all-purpose national feminist organization, which focused on developments in Washington, D.C. Throughout the 1970s, it made ratification of the embattled ERA its prime objective, to the neglect of other issues. In the 1980s and after, NOW turned its attention to the defense of abortion rights, effectively narrowing the public face of feminism. And because NOW emphasized electoral politics, it shaped its arguments to persuade a rightward-shifting government and so lost the radical edge that made earlier feminism so magnetic. None of this killed feminism, as media pundits loved to proclaim, but being on the defensive for so long, combined with feminists' own conflicts, took a toll on morale and active participation.

CARRYING ON IN A POLARIZED ERA

Still, feminist organizing continued and even reached into new arenas. As the direct action phase of the movement waned, women brought feminist ideas into the range of institutions that made up American society and reshaped them. Universities were transformed by the multiplication of Women's Studies programs and the infusion of gender analysis into established disciplines from history to biochemistry. Women's centers, gay-straight alliances, and AIDS action coalitions joined the panoply of student groups, bringing new ideas and energies into campus politics. The body-mind distinction, so foundational to historic patriarchy, gave way as women developed their intellects and physical strength. By 1980, girls made up one-third of all high school athletes. Their participation had multiplied sixfold since the early 1970s, thanks to feminist pressure, new federal requirements for gender equity, and girls' own eagerness to compete.

Lobbying pressure by groups such as NOW facilitated the appointment and promotion of women to important government positions. Many of those appointed were influenced by the women's movement.

(Opposite) **Figure 6.** *"Change Will Come," 1977*
Catholic sisters were among the founders of NOW in 1966, and women from various religious traditions became feminists. Active in the overall women's movement, they also challenged sexist theology and practices within their faiths. This nun was part of a 1977 demonstration at St. Patrick's Cathedral in New York calling for the ordination of women as priests.
Photo © by Bettye Lane. Reprinted with permission of Donna McAlpine.

Ruth Bader Ginsburg, for example, nominated to the Supreme Court by President Bill Clinton, had helped transform the nation's legal system as director of the Women's Rights Project of the American Civil Liberties Union before becoming a judge. She brought a feminist analysis to issues from affirmative action to military affairs. Even Sandra Day O'Connor, though appointed by Ronald Reagan, became a key swing vote on the Court in defense of feminist gains.

Feminists also altered their religious institutions, pushing for changes in theology, liturgy, and governance (see Document 27). Some trained for and sought ordination as ministers, rabbis, and priests. Among those who changed their church was Pauli Murray, the black feminist who was instrumental in including women in the equal employment clause of the 1964 Civil Rights Act. After a long struggle, Murray triumphed over what she called "a two-thousand-year tribal taboo" to achieve ordination as one of the first female Episcopal priests in 1977.[21] The Roman Catholic Church hierarchy helped lead the opposition to ERA, abortion, and gay rights, but it, too, encountered internal struggle. Catholic nuns and laywomen began organizing in the mid-1970s to challenge sexism and promote the ordination of women as priests (see Figure 6).

Even the military, the most avidly masculine major institution in American life, was altered by women. Participants in the Defense Advisory Committee on Women in the Armed Services pressed successfully to integrate the armed forces and make them act on sexual harassment and other forms of discrimination against servicewomen. The changes proved especially important to African American women and Latinas, who enlist in the military in large numbers in hopes of education funding and social mobility.

Ironically, even some conservative women took feminist stands. Jeane Kirkpatrick, appointed by President Reagan as the U.S. ambassador to the United Nations, openly bristled at official "sexism" in the 1980s. For fairness to prevail, she concluded, society would have to "abandon the notion, still supported by some religious denominations, that men are the natural governors of society, . . . [and] that femininity is inexorably associated with the submissiveness of female to male." "What must go," she continued, "is the expectation that the male will have prime responsibility for the financial support of the family and the female for its nurturance."[22] The policies of the organizations with which conservative women aligned remained resolutely antifeminist, and the Republican Party itself became more so between 1970 and the opening of the new century. But the growing discomfort of some female conservatives with open sexism suggested a cultural revolution that would be hard to reverse.

Meanwhile, as the highly visible protest stage of the women's movement waned, people who had been influenced by feminism moved into fields of activism that did not focus on women's issues per se. Scores of women developed their leadership skills at the Midwest Academy, which Heather Booth opened in 1973. A former SNCC activist, founder of the Jane abortion service, and a Chicago Women's Liberation Union member, Booth trained organizers for social, economic, and political justice at the academy. In the 1990s, women-led community development organizations worked to bring better housing, health care, and participatory democracy to low-income neighborhoods in cities from Las Vegas to Boston. Women also launched battles for environmental justice in the late 1970s and early 1980s, as they learned of the high rates of miscarriage, birth defects, and illness due to corporate toxic waste dumping in their communities. From Brownsville, Texas, to Chatham, North Carolina, to Woburn, Massachusetts, to San Jose, California, the movement spread as mothers compared notes and mobilized their communities to fight the polluters.

Nuclear power plants and nuclear weapons raised related concerns about health and even human survival, and veterans of feminism played key roles in these struggles, too. Leslie Cagan's story illustrates the evolution of female activist trajectories. Working in the movement to end the war in Vietnam in the 1960s, Cagan then turned her attention to the women's liberation movement, the lesbian and gay movement, and the abortion rights struggle. In the 1980s she moved into peace and disarmament work as a program coordinator for Mobilization for Survival, an alliance of more than 100 national and local organizations working to eliminate nuclear weapons and close nuclear power plants. In the new century, she helped lead United for Peace and Justice, a broad coalition of organizations against the U.S. war in Iraq and for social justice at home.

Others played vital roles in campaigns for human rights of other kinds. Maria Elena Durazo, for example, chaired the mobilization for the national Immigrant Workers Freedom Ride of 2004. The child of Mexican migrant farmworkers, Durazo became the first Latina to serve as president of a major union local in southern California. Now called UNITE HERE, her union organizes female housekeepers and other hotel workers and ties the labor movement to larger social justice efforts such as civil rights, lesbian and gay rights, and immigration reform (see Document 35).

Celebrating the wide-reaching ripples from the women's movement's splash, *Ms.* magazine produced a special anniversary issue in 1994 called "50 Ways to Be a Feminist." It included cameos of women in what seemed like every domain of human activity. No wonder a *Time* magazine poll in 1989 found that more than four out of five women believed that the women's movement had helped improve women's lives.

AMERICAN FEMINISTS ON A GLOBAL STAGE

Feminism took a quantum leap forward internationally after 1970, in part because the conditions that produced the movement in the United States were hardly unique. Growing life expectancy, declining birthrates, surging female labor force participation, greater separation of sexuality and reproduction, and broader access to education characterized many countries in the late twentieth century. New feminisms developed as women faced old problems with new resources. Among those resources was the ever more popular political tool of the nongovernmental organization (NGO). The number of NGOs grew from almost none in the late 1950s to 6,000 in 1990 to 26,000 at the century's end. Driving nearly all the progress that human rights made in world public opinion, NGOs influenced the work of the United Nations and provided vital services at the grassroots in many of its member countries.

In 1973, women-led NGOs at a Vienna United Nations conference won recognition that women's rights are part of "human rights." In 1975, constituting themselves as a tribune parallel to the main UN meeting, they won the establishment of the world Decade for Women. Thereafter, they brought gender-conscious analysis to global problems from poverty and pollution to health care and education. And they pushed for solutions based on gender equity as the only way to ensure sustainable economic development and encourage world peace. Thus, even as feminism's momentum slowed in the United States in the face of powerful opposition, it accelerated abroad (see Document 34).

Barely thirty years after the 1964 Civil Rights Act first outlawed sex discrimination in the United States, 7,000 Americans were among the 16,921 delegates in Beijing, China, representing governments from around the world at the 1995 World Women's Conference. Another 30,000 attended the parallel NGO forum. Women from developing countries assumed a leading role. Participants drew up plans for achieving global equality for women as they proclaimed justice for women and girls to be "in the interest of all humanity as an inalienable, integral, and indivisible part of universal rights." The delegates adopted a wide-ranging platform, yet stressed how "the increasing poverty that is affecting the majority of the world's people, in particular, women and children" demanded unprecedented creativity and cooperation across borders. Their mission statement announced that "equality between women and men is a matter of human rights and a condition for social justice and is also a necessary and fundamental prerequisite for equality, development, and peace" in the twenty-first century. Achieving such goals would prove much more difficult than articulating them, but the mere fact that such a wide array of people came together with this vision and with some backing from their governments marked the huge distance traversed over a half-century of activism (see Documents 39 and 40).

Back at home, a cohort of younger women set out to update feminism to meet the challenge of new conditions. The first generation born in the wake of the women's movement's greatest victories came of age in the 1990s, when the contradictions of the women's movement's unfinished revolution were startlingly apparent in American life (see Documents 37 and 40). They focused on issues of pressing concern to them, such as sexual exploration, subjectivity and self-image, diversity and inclusivity, and work-family balance. More unreservedly pro-sex than any previous generation, they were also more adventurous in exploring the meanings and pleasures of the body. Many embraced "queerness" as they drew attention to the variability and volatility of gender identification and sexual desire. Some adopted the mantle "third wave" to distinguish their views from the "second wave" feminists who had driven the changes of the 1960s and 1970s. In 1993, the writer Rebecca Walker set up the Third Wave Foundation to promote discussion and organize voter registration campaigns to draw young women into politics. Like their predecessors, the Third Wave feminists often disagreed over analysis, priorities, and strategies.

By the first years of the new century, some even questioned whether the metaphor of waves obscured more than it illuminated about the long women's movement. Lisa Jervis, a cofounder of *Bitch* magazine, a quintessential forum of youthful feminism, argued that the notion of a generational split between two waves of the movement was a media-driven myth that distorted a more complex reality. Feminists of every generation had divided among themselves over ideology and often allied with women (and men) of other age groups who shared their thinking and priorities, she pointed out. Jervis urged old and young alike to give up the fixation on waves of feminism, address their substantive differences, and, above all, join forces to concentrate on "the real work before the movement today."[23]

These debates over self-definition and future direction pointed to a deeper truth. More than 150 years after its emergence as a social movement, feminism was alive and well. As women in varied circumstances regularly reinterpreted it to meet the challenge of working for gender justice in a rapidly changing world, feminisms multiplied and changed but they seemed unlikely to disappear before their work was done.

NOTES

[1]Sarah H. Grimké, *Letters on the Equality of the Sexes and Other Essays*, ed. Elizabeth Ann Bartlett (New Haven, Conn.: Yale University Press, 1988), 35.

[2]Nancy F. Gabin, *Feminism in the Labor Movement: Women and the United Auto Workers, 1935–1975* (Ithaca, N.Y.: Cornell University Press, 1990), 188.

[3]Dorothy Sue Cobble, *The Other Women's Movement: Workplace Justice and Social Rights in Modern America* (Princeton, N.J.: Princeton University Press, 2004), 3.

[4]John D'Emilio, *Lost Prophet: The Life and Times of Bayard Rustin* (New York: Free Press, 2003), 351–52.

[5]Charles Payne, *I've Got the Light of Freedom: The Organizing Tradition and the Mississippi Freedom Struggle* (Berkeley: University of California Press, 1995), 138.

[6]Nan Alamilla Boyd, *Wide Open Town: A History of Queer San Francisco to 1965* (Berkeley: University of California Press, 2003), 150–51, 177.

[7]Brett Harvey, *The Fifties: A Women's Oral History* (New York: HarperCollins, 1993), 226.

[8]Stephanie Coontz, *Marriage, a History: From Obedience to Intimacy* (New York: Viking, 2005), passim, pill data on 254; Gerda Lerner, *Why History Matters* (New York: Oxford University Press, 1997), 97.

[9]Gabin, *Feminism in the Labor Movement*, 2, 121.

[10]Sara Evans, *Personal Politics: The Roots of Women's Liberation in the Civil Rights Movement and the New Left* (New York: Random House, 1979), 221.

[11]Jessie Lopez De La Cruz interview in Ellen Cantarow, *Moving the Mountain: Women Working for Social Change* (Boston: Feminist Press, 1980), 134, 136–37.

[12]*Women's Role in Contemporary Society: The Report of the New York City Commission on Human Rights, September 21–25, 1970* (New York: Avon Books, 1972), 54–55, 57.

[13]Lillian Faderman, *Odd Girls and Twilight Lovers: A History of Lesbian Life in Twentieth-Century America* (New York: Columbia University Press, 1991), 213.

[14]Jennifer Nelson, *Women of Color and the Reproductive Rights Movement* (New York: New York University Press, 2003), 133.

[15]Barbara Smith, *The Truth That Never Hurts: Writings on Race, Gender, and Freedom* (New Brunswick, N.J.: Rutgers University Press, 1998), 96.

[16]Sara Evans, *Tidal Wave: How Women Changed America at Century's End* (New York: Free Press, 2003), 37.

[17]On the porous boundaries and prevalence of coalition away from big-city media centers, see Stephanie Gilmore, ed., *Feminist Coalitions: Historical Perspectives on Second-*

Wave Feminism in the United States (Urbana: University of Illinois Press, 2008); and Stephanie Gilmore, *Groundswell: Grassroots Feminism in Postwar America* (forthcoming, 2009).

[18]Barbara Ehrenreich, *The Hearts of Men: American Dreams and the Flight from Commitment* (New York: Anchor Books, 1983), 145.

[19]Susan Faludi, *Backlash: The Undeclared War against American Women* (New York: Crown, 1991), 237.

[20]Ibid., 235.

[21]Pauli Murray, *Pauli Murray: The Autobiography of a Black Activist, Feminist, Lawyer, Priest, and Poet* (Knoxville: University of Tennessee Press, 1989), 430.

[22]Quoted in Rebecca Klatch, "Coalition and Conflict among Women of the New Right," *Signs* 13 (Summer 1988): 680; and Toni Carabillo, Judith Meuli, June Bundy Csida, *Feminist Chronicles: 1953–1993* (Los Angeles: Women's Graphics, 1993), 114.

[23]Lisa Jervis, "The End of Feminism's Third Wave," *Ms.* (Winter 2004–2005): 56–58.

The Documents

The Doctrine

1

CONGRESS OF AMERICAN WOMEN

The Position of the American Woman Today
1946

After women won the right to vote in 1920, efforts to improve women's standing and win other important reforms continued. Activists worked through labor organizations, the National Consumers League, the National Council of Negro Women, the YWCA, and a host of other groups. As World War II ended, this grassroots infrastructure facilitated a broad-based coalition called Congress of American Women (CAW). After the cold war Red Scare decimated CAW, some participants found other ways to advance their commitments. A case in point was Gerda Lerner, then a housewife, who went on to pioneer the study of women's history in the United States two decades later.

The American woman of today is a vastly different person from her 19th century predecessor. She is unlike her mother who matured and married before World War I. Yet she is the product of these women — she has inherited their successes and failures. The economic collapse of the 1930's, . . . the constant "pump priming" of the period as the government struggled to keep the economy from a complete breakdown, developed a new type of woman. The American woman entered World War II hardened and tempered by her experiences during the Great Depression. She had known confusion and chaos, had suffered unemployment, bread lines, evictions; she had learned the value of united, political action in the common good. . . .

The terrible manpower needs of the Second World War . . . opened the doors of basic industry . . . wide to women for the first time. . . . By 1944 the number [of women in American industry] had increased to 17 million, women constituting 32.5% of the entire labor force.

Communism, Socialism, and Radical Left Politics Collection, Sophia Smith Collection, Smith College, Northampton, MA.

The most marked change in the composition of the female labor force is the number of married and older women who are now working. . . . Although the manpower shortage of the Second World War increased women's total earnings, this was primarily due to longer hours. Even during the period when women were most in demand, they did not receive equal pay for equal work.

American women went into the armed forces and into the auxiliary services; women did jobs that left old army men aghast. They worked on the railroads, as mechanics and technicians. They did the "dirty work" and the heavy work, and were paid less for doing it, as part of the most magnificent demonstration of social production in American history.

Yet it is significant that none of the "Fair Employment Practices" legislation which came into being during the war included discrimination because of sex. . . . This unrealistic approach to the problems of working women was characteristic of America's war effort. The foremost and compelling problem of the working mother has always been adequate day care for her children. While the War Manpower Commission was carrying on national campaigns to get more women into war work, the question of child care was given belated consideration only after many serious accidents to children left alone while their mother worked. . . .

But as a result of the lessons of the war, American women of today . . . are more aware of themselves as part of the world. . . . The Congress of American Women, affiliated with the Women's International Democratic Federation, makes it possible to unite the middle class women's groups with the working women's organizations and the trade unions. . . .

Just prior to V. J. [Victory in Japan] Day, the Women's Bureau of the U.S. Department of Labor conducted a survey of 13,000 women workers in 10 metropolitan areas to discuss their postwar plans. The report revealed the heavy financial and economic responsibilities of American women. . . . Seventy-five percent of all women questioned reported that they must continue to work, and reported that they would like to remain in industry rather than return to service or other occupations. Of the women surveyed . . . 15% were the only wage earners in the family. In addition to economic responsibility, 8 out of every 100 women worked to free the family from debt, to educate the children, to help own a home. . . .

[Yet] in the immediate cut-back of war production following V-J Day women workers suffered lay-offs more serious than that of other groups. . . .

Of all women the American Negro women have been hit hardest. Job opportunities opened to women during the war were not available to them, except in the dirtiest and lowest-paying groups. Now many of these Negro women have been forced back into domestic service. . . .

The problem of the working woman . . . does not end with equal pay, equal upgrading or the end of discrimination in employment. Freedom to work means freedom to do two full-time jobs. A New York State Department of Labor Study attributed wartime breakdown in women's health to the fact that they worked a full shift in industry or office and then went home to another full day's work, cooking, cleaning, washing, mending. Long hours and night work took their toll of woman's strength, but the disproportionate burdens the working mother or wife is required to assume took a higher toll. Lack of help, not lack of physical ability, is the apex of the problem—the American woman has been found capable of doing most jobs as well as men, but her difficulties arise when she tries to do two jobs as well as the man does only one.

Politically the American woman of today is only "half awake." In the major political parties most of the difficult detail work is done by the women of the parties, yet the number of woman candidates is small, and women are still nominated as a "token" of respect rather than out of recognition of their abilities. Twenty-six years after the American woman secured the right to vote, with a numerical voting superiority, . . . only seven women are in the House of Representatives and four in the Senate. . . . Both the Republican and Democratic Parties pass pious resolutions about "equal rights," . . . yet these political organizations are dominated and controlled by men, and have shown very little understanding of the problems of women. Women are now becoming aware of the necessity of united political action, and for the election of more women to office. The Congress of American Women plans to fight for "48 Women in Congress in '48."

Legally, too, the American woman is only "half free." The old hangovers of the common law principles have led to some feudal discriminations which are still enforced in the states. For example, in . . . 15 states a woman can become the natural guardian of her child only if it is born out of wedlock, but in three of those states she can go to jail if she does not reveal the name of the father, in which case he becomes the guardian. In four states the rights of a woman to make a contract are limited; in five states her right to convey real property does not exist. In eight states the husband controls all of the property of the marriage without regard for the contributions of the wife. In five states court authorizations are necessary for a married woman to conduct a business, and three more require this authority plus the written consent of the husband for her to keep her earnings from such business. In six states she is not entitled to her wages—they belong to her husband as part of the marriage property. In three states a married woman's will is automatically revoked by her marriage. . . .

Until the day when the American woman is free to develop her mind and abilities to their fullest extent, without discrimination because of her sex, is free to work without neglecting her children, to live with her husband on an equal level, with adequate provision made for the care [of] that home without injury to her health; until she takes her full responsibilities as citizen and individual, supporting herself if necessary and her family where she has a family, at a decent wage, paid equally with men for the work she does; until she is freed from the terror of war, and lives in a world of peaceful friendship between nations, in a society without prejudice against Negro, Jew, national groups or women—her long struggle for emancipation must continue.

The Commission on the Status of Women of the Congress of American Women pledges itself to continue to unite women in America around such objectives, to the support of labor, of international peace and democracy, and for the improvement of the conditions of women the world over.

2

EDITH M. STERN

Women Are Household Slaves

1949

Even at the height of the cold war, dissent and radical social criticism endured. Publishing her piece in a popular magazine known for its satirical edge, the writer and mental health expert Edith M. Stern drew attention to the drudgery that characterized the lives of housewives. Her contrast between regulations that protected workers' rights in industry

The American Mercury 68, no. 301 (January 1949): 71–76.

and women's vulnerability in the home suggests how union organizing and New Deal reforms emboldened politically minded American women to seek to better their own situation.

HELP WANTED: DOMESTIC: FEMALE. All cooking, cleaning, laundering, sewing, meal planning, shopping, weekday chauffering, social secretarial service, and complete care of three children. Salary at employer's option. Time off if possible.

No one in her right senses would apply for such a job. No one in his right senses, even a desperate widower, would place such an advertisement. Yet it correctly describes the average wife and mother's situation, in which most women remain for love, but many because they have no way out.

A nauseating amount of bilge is constantly being spilled all over the public press about the easy, pampered existence of the American woman. Actually, the run of the mill, not gainfully employed female who is blessed with a husband and from two to four children leads a kind of life that theoretically became passé with the Emancipation Proclamation. . . .

Housewifery is a complex of housekeeping, household management, housework and childcare. Some of its elements, such as budgeting, dietetics, and above all, the proper upbringing of children, involve the higher brain centers. . . . Others of its facets, and those the most persistent and time-consuming, can be capably handled by an eight-year-old child. . . .

Organized labor and government afford workers certain standardized legal or customary protections. But in terms of enlightened labor practice, the housewife stands out blackly as the Forgotten Worker.

She is covered by no minimum wage law; indeed, she gets no wages at all. Like the bondservant of another day, or the slave, she receives maintenance; but anything beyond that, whether in the form of a regular "allowance" or sporadic largesse, is ruggedly individualistic. . . .

No state or county health and sanitation inspectors invade the privacy of the home, as they do that of the factory; hence kitchens and domestic dwellings may be ill-ventilated, unsanitary and hazardous without penalty. That many more accidents occur in homes than in industry is no coincidence. Furthermore, when a disability is incurred, such as a bone broken in a fall off a ladder or legs scalded by the overturning of a kettle of boiling water, no beneficent legislation provides for the housewife's compensation.

Rest periods are irregular, about ten to fifteen minutes each, a few times during the long day; night work is frequent and unpredictably occasioned by a wide variety of factors such as the mending basket, the gang gathering for a party, a sick child, or even more pressing, a sick husband. The right to a vacation, thoroughly accepted in business and industry, is non-existent in the domestic sphere. When families go to beach bungalows or shacks in the woods Mom continues on almost the same old treadmill; . . . three meals a day to prepare, beds to be made and dishes to be washed. . . .

Though progressive employers make some sort of provision for advancement, the housewife's opportunities for advancement are nil; the nature and scope of her job, the routines of keeping a family fed, clothed and housed remain always the same. If the male upon whom her scale of living depends prospers, about all to which she can look forward is a large house—and more work. . . .

Despite all this, a good many arguments about the joys of house-wifery have been advanced, largely by those who have never had to work at it. One much stressed point is the satisfaction every good woman feels in creating a home for her dear ones. Well, probably every good woman does feel it, perhaps because she has had it so drummed into her that if she does not, she is not a good woman; but that satisfaction has very little to do with housewifery and housework. It is derived from intangibles, such as the desirable wife-husband and mother-child relationships she manages to effect, the permeating general home atmosphere of joviality or hospitality or serenity or culture to which she is the key, or the warmth and security she gives to the home by way of her personality, not her broom, stove or dishpan. . . .

According to another line of unreasoning, the housewife has the advantage of being "her own boss" and unlike the gainfully employed worker can arrange her own schedules. This is pure balderdash, despite the fact that she may suit herself about such minor matters as whether she is going to make the beds in the morning or let them go until the afternoon, elect Thursday rather than Friday for closet clean-ing. If there is anything more inexorable than children's needs, from an infant's yowls of hunger and Junior's shrieks that he has just fallen down the stairs to the subtler need of an adolescent for a good listener during one of his or her frequent emotional crises, it is only the pres-sure of Dad's demand for supper as soon as he gets home. . . . What is more, not her own preferences as to hours, but those set by her husband's office or plant, by the schools, by pediatricians and dentists, and the children's homework establish when the housewife rises, when she goes forth, and when she cannot get to bed. . . .

The housewife . . . carries through each complex operation of cooking, cleaning, tidying and laundering solo; almost uniquely among workers since the Industrial Revolution, she does not benefit by division of labor. Lunch time, ordinarily a pleasant break in the working day, for her brings no pleasant sociability with the girls in the cafeteria, the hired men in the shade of the haystack, or even the rest of the household staff in the servants' dining room. From the time her husband departs for work until he returns, except for an occasional chat across the back fence or a trek to market . . . she lacks adult company; and even to the most passionately maternal, unbroken hours of childish prattle are no substitute for the conversation of one's peers, whether that be on a high philosophical plane or on the lower level of neighborhood gossip. . . .

When a man marries and has children, it is assumed that he will do the best work along lines in which he has been trained or is at least interested. When a woman marries and has children, it is assumed that she will take to housewifery. But whether she takes to it or not, she does it.

Such regimentation, for professional or potentially professional women, is costly both for the individual and society. For the individual, it brings about conflicts and frustrations. The practice of housewifery gives the lie to the theory of almost every objective of higher education. The educated individual should have a community, a national, a world viewpoint; but that is pretty difficult to get and hold when you are continually involved with cleaning toilets, ironing shirts, peeling potatoes, darning socks and minding children. The educated should read widely; but reading requires time and concentration and besides, the conscientious housewife has her own five-foot shelf of recipes and books on child psychology to occupy her. . . .

Buried in the homemade cakes the family loves, lost among the stitches of patches, sunk in the suds of the week's wash, are incalculable skilled services.

But just as slaves were in the service of individual masters, not of the community or state or nation in general, so are housewives bound to the service of individual families. That it devolves upon a mother to tend her children during helpless infancy and childhood—or at any rate, to see that they are tended by someone—is undeniable. But only a psychology of slavery can put women at the service of grown men. Ironically, the very gentlemen scrupulous about opening a door for a lady, carrying her packages, or helping her up onto a curb, take it for granted that at mealtimes, all their lives long, ladies should carry their food to them and never sit through a meal while they never get up. A wife, when she picks up the soiled clothing her husband has strewn on the floor, lugs his garments to the tailor, makes his twin bed, or sews on his buttons, acts as an unpaid body-servant. If love is the justification for this role, so was love a justification for antebellum Mammies. Free individuals, in a democracy, perform personal services for themselves or, if they have the cash, pay other free individuals to wait on them. It is neither freedom nor democracy when such service is based on color or sex.

3

UNITED AUTO WORKERS

A Union Protects Its Women Members

1955

Even as American politics became more conservative in the late 1940s and 1950s, some progressive organizations with a large proportion of women members continued to make advances. Among these were trade unions affiliated with the Congress of Industrial Organizations (CIO), such as the United Auto Workers. Many women had obtained jobs in the auto industry during World War II, and those who managed to stay employed into the 1950s became an important minority within the union. This 1955 convention debate over a resolution to fight discrimination based on sex and marital status reveals the contrasting ways working people responded to the breakdown of the male-breadwinner-based family-wage system. It also illustrates how women used union principles and civil rights arguments to advance their quest for equality.

Proceedings, 15th Annual Convention, Union of Auto, Aerospace and Agricultural Implement Workers of America (UAW-CIO), Cleveland Public Auditorium, March 27, 1955–April 1, 1955, pp. 52–57, 61–62. Reprinted in Gerda Lerner, *The Female Experience: An American Documentary* (Indianapolis: Bobbs-Merrill, 1977), 309–16.

DELEGATE LOVELAND, LOCAL 174: I rise to speak in favor of this resolution. . . . We all know that employers discriminate against women more
than any other group. In my own particular plant, to my knowledge
they haven't hired a woman in the factory since 1944, even though they
did hire quite a few employees in 1950. . . .

While I have the floor I would like to express my opinion on married women working. I don't think that any of the delegates in this
room have the right to challenge the necessity of two incomes, and
I don't think it is too much of our business. I also say that I believe
married women work only because they have to, the majority of them.
Therefore, I urge the adoption of this resolution.

DELEGATE BERRY, LOCAL 835: I urge the adoption of this resolution
for the reason that there are too many women that work merely
because they are the breadwinners for the family. In the case of Negro
women if they don't work in the plant they are then forced to go out
and do day work [domestic service] for $6 a day and carfare. In some
instances that I personally know about some of them are taking care
of crippled husbands and a lot of children that nobody else will help
support. I urge the adoption of this resolution. . . .

DELEGATE CARRIGAN, LOCAL 887: In my Local there are approximately 2,000 women members, and in a group that size we find practically all the problems you will find in any given set of workers who
have discrimination at the hiring gate and then promotion and termination. . . . Many of us have ten or more years of seniority in our jobs
and are still in the lowest classifications. . . .

The resolution states that an average income is 44 per cent less for
women than for men. This 44 per cent represents purchasing power
which should be in the workers' pockets instead of in management's
till. . . .

DELEGATE DRENNON, LOCAL 662: Brother Chairman, I am in support of this resolution. In our Local we have a real problem with this.
There are over 14,000 people working in our plants. Over 4,000 of
them are women. In many cases they do identical work with the men
and draw 16 cents less an hour. We feel that is wrong and we intend to
do something about it. . . .

DELEGATE HILL, LOCAL 961: Mr. Chairman, fellow delegates and sister delegates: I rise to oppose the particular resolution on the floor
at this time for the simple reason that I think that our International Union is trying to create a condition whereby it will require two

paychecks in every home in order that we might live like decent human beings. . . .

How about the poor fellow who has a big family and his wife has to stay at home and take care of those kids in order that there won't be juvenile delinquency, and there is only one paycheck coming into that home? That fellow simply cannot keep pace with the two paychecks. . . .

I am not opposed to single women and widows working in the shop, but I am opposed to married women working. . . .

DELEGATE EMMA MURPHY, LOCAL 3: . . . Year after year we come to convention, and the same resolution is passed every time. We are just giving lip service to the women in industry. . . .

Certainly I am in favor of the resolution, but let's do something about it and not just say we are going to and forget about it.

I am sort of burned up at some of the previous speakers, and I would like to get one of them in a debate where I could just talk back and forth to him. Two paychecks in a family are fine. I happen to be married. My husband happens to be one of those unfortunate people with 22 years seniority in Hudson Local Union No. 154. Today he has no job. What would happen if I wasn't able to work? My family would be going hungry. . . .

DELEGATE RUTT, LOCAL 195: . . . The trouble today is that married people, as I see it, want everything. They want a car, a home, a TV. You can't do that on one weekly pay, I will admit. They are not prepared to do as we did 30 or 40 years ago. . . . True, we didn't have everything we needed then. We haven't got everything we need today. But as long as there are single women looking for jobs the married woman's place is in the home. . . . As long as the husband is working it is his place to provide for his wife and family.

DELEGATE SZUR, LOCAL 174: I have been warned by my delegation first to watch my language, so with a tremendous effort I will try very hard.

In the first place, I would like to say give us good-looking men with enough money and we don't have to work.

But to get down and be real serious about it, who is to say a woman should work or should not? Where is our democracy in this country if a woman cannot be a free individual and make up her own mind? I think that when you start telling women you can or cannot work you are infringing upon their civil rights, which I as a woman resent.

I am not ashamed of some of the various speakers. They are union people, but I am disgusted with them. One of the brothers spoke about women working. I would like to ask that brother what he would do if he had the finances and wanted to start a business, and some other guy said, "You can't do it because you haven't got five kids; you have got to have five or you can't start a business." . . . If they told him he couldn't have a business, he would blow his fuse. . . .

We women helped organize this Union. We pay our dues; we attend our meetings, and many of us stand up to management better than some of our weak-spined brothers. . . .

We walk the picket line in the ice and snow—and I did at General Motors as long as we had the strike and I haven't forgotten it, and believe me I am willing to do it again. . . .

I am not married—happily. And I want to stay that way, believe it or not. But I say that a woman who works and leaves her children at home, a normal, good mother, sees that they have adequate care. It is not the quantity of the time they spend with the children; it is the quality of the training they give them while they are with them.

I say that a working mother is not a bad mother, any more than a mother who does not work and spends her time at bridge clubs and leaves her kids with somebody else. . . .

PRESIDENT REUTHER: . . . I would like to say . . . that a lot of people have substituted emotion for what the resolution calls for. . . . I come from a family that, thank God, had a mother who stayed home and took care of her children. But there are good mothers and there are bad mothers, and there are good fathers and bad fathers.

What we are talking about is if a woman is working whether we are going to protect her rights. That is a decision that people of a free country make. But where people are working who are women, are we going to protect their standards, are we going to permit management to exploit them and use them to undermine our standards? That is what we are dealing with here. So we ought to understand that.

Now, on the resolution which says that we will protect women workers against discrimination by appropriate contract provisions, all those in favor of that motion signify by saying aye; those opposed [nay].

The resolution is carried overwhelmingly.

4

DAUGHTERS OF BILITIS

Purpose of the Daughters of Bilitis
1955

In the postwar period, lesbians organized publicly for the first time, taking heart from African American civil rights efforts. In 1947, Edythe Eyde, a secretary in California, issued the country's first lesbian periodical, Vice Versa. When publishers refused to print it, she made carbon copies of each typescript issue. In 1955, four lesbian couples in San Francisco launched the Daughters of Bilitis (DOB), a lesbian civil rights group. Two of the leaders, Del Martin and Phyllis Lyon, were to play prominent roles in the wider women's movement of subsequent decades. They were the first same-sex couple to marry under San Francisco's new civil marriage law in 2004, celebrating more than fifty years of commitment.

A WOMEN'S ORGANIZATION FOR THE PURPOSE OF PROMOTING
THE INTEGRATION OF THE HOMOSEXUAL INTO SOCIETY BY:

1. Education of the variant, with particular emphasis on the psychological, physiological and sociological aspects, to enable her to understand herself and make her adjustment to society in all its social, civic and economic implications—this to be accomplished by establishing and maintaining as complete a library as possible of both fiction and nonfiction literature on the sex deviant theme; by sponsoring public discussions on pertinent subjects to be conducted by leading members of the legal, psychiatric, religious and other professions; by advocating a mode of behavior and dress acceptable to society.
2. Education of the public at large through acceptance first of the individual, leading to an eventual breakdown of erroneous conceptions, taboos and prejudices; through public discussion

The Ladder 1, no. 6 (March 1957): 2.

meetings aforementioned; through dissemination of educational literature on the homosexual theme.

3. Participation in research projects by duly authorized and responsible psychology, sociology and other such experts directed toward further knowledge of the homosexual.

4. Investigation of the penal code as it pertains to the homosexual, proposal of changes to provide an equitable handling of cases involving this minority group, and promotion of these changes through due process of law in the state legislatures.

5

ELLA BAKER

"Developing Leadership among Other People" in Civil Rights

*1960**

Rarely benefiting from the family wage, black women were more likely than white women to work outside the home and to assume leadership roles in their communities. The lifelong activist Ella Baker began organizing in Harlem in the 1930s, later became the director of branches for the National Association for the Advancement of Colored People (NAACP), and then became the first staffer of the Southern Christian Leadership Conference, where she worked with the Reverend Martin Luther King Jr. Concerned over the hierarchy and male domination in these civil rights organizations, she encouraged young activists who had participated in the lunch counter sit-ins of 1960 to build an independent Student Nonviolent Coordinating Committee (SNCC). Its motto, "Let the people decide," reflected her radical democratic philosophy.

*The dates for Documents 5, 6, and 11 reflect the years in which the primary historical events to which they refer occurred. These oral histories were collected years later and thus reflect the benefit of hindsight.

Gerda Lerner, *Black Women in White America: A Documentary History* (New York: Vintage, 1972), 346–52.

In my organizational work, I have never thought in terms of my "making a contribution." I just thought of myself as functioning where there was a need. And if I have made a contribution I think it may be that I had some influence on a large number of people.

As assistant field secretary of the branches of the NAACP, much of my work was in the South. At that time the NAACP was the leader on the cutting edge of social change. I remember when NAACP membership in the South was the basis for getting beaten up or even killed.

I used to leave New York about the 15th of February and travel through the South for four to five months. I would go to, say, Birmingham, Alabama, and help to organize membership campaigns. And in the process of helping to organize membership campaigns, there was opportunity for developing community reaction. You would go into areas where people were not yet organized in the NAACP and try to get them more involved. Maybe you would start with some simple thing like the fact that they had no street lights, or the fact that in the given area somebody had been arrested or had been jailed in a manner that was considered illegal and unfair, and the like. You would deal with whatever the local problem was, and on the basis of the needs of the people you would try to organize them in the NAACP.

Black people who were living in the South were constantly living with violence. Part of the job was to help them to understand what that violence was and how they in an organized fashion could help to stem it. The major job was getting people to understand that they had something within their power that they could use, and it could only be used if they understood what was happening and how group action could counter violence even when it was perpetrated by the police or, in some instances, the state. My basic sense of it has always been to get people to understand that in the long run they themselves are the only protection they have against violence or injustice. If they only had ten members in the NAACP at a given point, those ten members could be in touch with twenty-five members in the next little town, with fifty in the next and throughout the state as a result of the organization of state conferences, and they, of course, could be linked up with the national. People have to be made to understand that they cannot look for salvation anywhere but to themselves.

Come 1957, I went down South a couple of times in connection with the formation of the Southern Christian Leadership Conference. . . . I went down with the idea of not spending more than six weeks there, giving myself a month to get the thing going, and then two weeks to clean it up. I stayed with SCLC for two and a half years, because they didn't have anybody. My official capacity was varied. When I first went down, I didn't insist on a title, which is nothing new or unusual for me; it didn't bother me. . . . I kept on until the summer of 1960. And prior to that, of course, the sit-ins had started, and I was able to get the SCLC to at least sponsor the conference in Raleigh. We had hoped to call together about 100 or 125 of the young leaders who had emerged in the sit-ins in the South. But of course the sit-ins had been so dynamic in the field that when we got to the meeting we had two hundred and some people, including some from the North. And out of that conference of the Easter weekend of 1960, which I coordinated and organized, we had a committee that came out of it, and out of that committee SNCC was born.

And after SNCC came into existence, of course, it opened up a new era of struggle. I felt the urge to stay close by. Because if I had done anything anywhere, it had been largely in the role of supporting things, and in the background of things that needed to be done for the organizations that were supposedly out front. So I felt if I had done it for the elders, I could do it for young people.

I had no difficulty relating to the young people. I spoke their language in terms of the meaning of what they had to say. . . .

There are those, some of the young people especially, who have said to me that if I had not been a woman I would have been well known in certain places, and perhaps held certain kinds of positions.

I have always felt it was a handicap for oppressed peoples to depend so largely upon a leader, because unfortunately in our culture, the charismatic leader usually becomes a leader because he has found a spot in the public limelight. It usually means he has been touted through the public media, which means that the media made him, and the media may undo him. There is also the danger in our culture that, because a person is called upon to give public statements and is acclaimed by the establishment, such a person gets to the point of believing that he *is* the movement. Such people get so involved with playing the game of being important that they exhaust themselves and their time, and they don't do the work of actually organizing people.

For myself, circumstances frequently dictated what had to be done as I saw it. For example, I had no plans to go down and set up the office of SCLC. But it seemed unless something were done whatever impetus had been gained would be lost, and nobody else was available who was willing or able to do it. So I went because to me it was more important to see what was a potential for all of us than it was to do what I might have done for myself. I knew from the beginning that as a woman, an older woman, in a group of ministers who are accustomed to having women largely as supporters, there was no place for me to have come into a leadership role. The competition wasn't worth it.

The movement of the '50's and '60's was carried largely by women, since it came out of church groups. . . . The number of women who carried the movement is much larger than that of men. Black women have had to carry this role, and I think the younger women are insisting on an equal footing.

. . . I think that certainly the young people who are challenging this ought to be challenging it, and it ought to be changed. But I also think you have to have a certain sense of your own value, and a sense of security on your part, to be able to forgo the glamor of what the leadership role offers. From the standpoint of my work and my own self-concepts, I don't think I have thought of myself largely as a woman. I thought of myself as an individual with a certain amount of sense of the need of people to participate in the movement. I have always thought what is needed is the development of people who are interested not in *being* leaders as much as in *developing* leadership among other people. Every time I see a young person who has come through the system to a stage where he could profit from the system and identify with it, but who identifies more with the struggle of black people who have not had his chance, every time I find such a person I take new hope. I feel a new life as a result of it.

6

ETHOL BAROL TAYLOR

"There Was Such a Feeling of Sisterhood"
in Working for Peace

1962

In 1961, over 50,000 women joined a new organization, Women's Strike for Peace (WSP), to campaign against the arms race and nuclear testing. Among the members was Ethel Barol Taylor, who, like many of the members, was a homemaker. Standing on their responsibility as mothers to ensure the well-being of their children, WSP members built popular support for the Nuclear Test Ban Treaty of 1963. This oral history reveals how motherhood could be a politicizing force and the much-stereotyped suburbs a site of community building for change. Taylor's story demonstrates how the "ladylike" manner of WSP members threw their conservative critics in the House Un-American Activities Committee off guard and so helped to legitimate dissent in the waning days of McCarthyism.

I was catapulted into the peace movement with the dropping of the bomb on Hiroshima. I was pretty apolitical up to that point. I used to get up in the morning and start polishing the furniture until I was polishing the polish. I thought, "There must be more to life than this."

I had a daughter, who was a small child at the time of the bombing of Hiroshima. When I read that the blast was so hot that in some circumstances it incinerated people and left just a shadow against a stone wall, creating instant fossils, I was numbed. I realized there were wars and there were wars, but this kind of war must never happen again.

There were others who felt as I did, and a few of us got together and talked. We formed a little group of women to study issues. I think even then, even though I was not political, I had this feeling that because women are not in positions of power and they have no role in policymaking, that maybe what we had to do was to make policy outside of government and demand of government that it listen to us.

Oral history transcript in Judith Porter Adams, *Peacework: Oral Histories of Women Peace Activists* (Boston: Twayne Publishers, 1991), 11–18. Original interview recording housed at Stanford University's Archive of Recorded Sound in the Women's International League for Peace and Freedom Collection, Collection Number ARS.0056.

... In the early days of Women Strike for Peace, women in the demonstrations, who were generally middle-class women, wore white gloves and hats. We used to do things like sit down and not move in the middle of the street, or whatever, but we would have our hats and white gloves on. I always thought that was a real protection until once we had an action, and hundreds of people went to Washington as a symbolic takeover of Congress. We walked and we came to a narrow street. The police said, "Cross this street and you get arrested." Well, I realized then that, what could they do? They're not going to electrocute me. They're not going to shoot me. It was much easier to cross that street than not to cross that street, so I crossed that street. Then we sat on the ground and waited to be arrested. We sat down, but we decided we weren't going to be yanked by our armpits, we were going to walk like ladies to the police van. We did. We got to the jail, and they opened the back door of the van. I looked out, and there was a five-foot drop to the ground. I waited for the policeman to help me down. The policeman came around and said, "Jump, sister." So I jumped into an entirely new world.

... We started because of children, because the scientists and doctors said that the strontium 90 and iodine 131 from the atomic tests would poison our children's milk and cause cancer. When we first organized we sent out a call throughout the streets with leaflets saying, "Take your children off milk." We sent our children's baby teeth to a lab in St. Louis to determine if strontium 90 was present. We were concerned about an epidemic, like polio before vaccines, except that polio is viral and these were man-made epidemics. Those who were then children now have children themselves.

My work in Women Strike for Peace sustains me. Outside of my family and my friends, WSP to me is the most important entity. It started out as a one-day action. We would meet every week around my dining room table to plan our "strike." There was a sugar bowl in the middle of the table for contributions toward the action. Some women stopped going to the hairdresser and did their own hair and put the money in the bowl. Some put birthday checks in. In one remarkable case, a woman who had very little money would occasionally give blood to the Red Cross and put the five dollars in the bowl. There was a wonderful outpouring of feeling and sisterhood. We were the harbingers of the women's movement—our weekly round table discussions were certainly consciousness raising. It was really an amazing experience. . . .

In 1962 some WSP members were brought before the House Un-American Activities Committee [HUAC]. In order to show solidarity, many of us wrote to the chair of the committee asking for an opportunity to testify. The hearing was in 1962. It was pure theater. There is a wonderful cartoon about the HUAC hearings and WSP. There are these two guys sitting up at the HUAC table, and one of them says, "What are we against, women or peace?" They were against both. When some of us walked in, the guards were standing out in the hall outside the hearing room minding baby carriages and babies. We all carried red roses, and each time a woman would step down from testifying, we would present her with a bouquet, and we would applaud. The committee kept threatening to clear the room. They were in real trouble! They couldn't get out of the sessions, and they became more and more permissive because we were all so good-natured. The committee was just ridiculed away. It was a tremendous victory against the hearings.

When Dagmar Wilson was asked if there were Communists in WSP, she responded very pleasantly by saying something like, "We welcome everyone as long as they are for disarmament." That was quite a statement to make. . . . These were middle-class women whose jobs did not depend on whether or not they were cleared by this committee. I'm sure the HUAC experience for the women questioned was pretty scary, but the great difference was the tremendous, enthusiastic support they received publicly. We had a clipping service of all of the newspapers that covered the hearings. It was all "hats off to the ladies," as I remember.

In 1975 President Ford appointed a commission on CIA activities within the United States. We learned things that amazed us. We learned that the CIA paid women, mostly housewives, one hundred dollars a week to infiltrate WSP. We suspected it at the time, but we didn't know. These women were instructed by the CIA to attend meetings, to show an interest in the purpose of the organization, and to make modest financial contributions, but not to exercise any leadership. It was a perfect cover; that describes half our membership—they don't want leadership roles, and they don't give too much money. The CIA also opened our mail. When we learned this we immediately instituted a suit against the CIA; we sued for surveillance, infiltration, and for mail opening. The first two charges were dropped, but they settled out of court for mail opening and gave us five thousand dollars. It wasn't so much money, but what a sweet moral victory! We used part of the money for our campaign to abolish the CIA.

7

PRESIDENT'S COMMISSION
ON THE STATUS OF WOMEN

Invitation to Action

1963

In 1961, the U.S. Women's Bureau, founded in 1920, persuaded President John F. Kennedy to create the President's Commission on the Status of Women (PCSW). To staff it, he selected twenty-six members, among them leaders of several long-standing mass-based women's organizations. To chair the commission, Kennedy chose former first lady Eleanor Roosevelt, whose prestige and connections with women's activist networks reached back to the Progressive Era. The commission's 1963 report strongly criticized sex and race discrimination and made recommendations for change in a wide range of arenas. It also catalyzed the formation of state and local commissions on the status of women that became a vital nucleus of the feminist movement. Many commission members went on to found the National Organization for Women in 1966.

This report is an invitation to action. When President John F. Kennedy appointed our Commission, he said: ... *we have by no means done enough to strengthen family life and at the same time encourage women to make their full contribution as citizens. . . . It is appropriate at this time . . . to review recent accomplishments, and to acknowledge frankly the further steps that must be taken. This is a task for the entire Nation.*

The 96 million American women and girls include a range from infant to octogenarian, from migrant farm mother to suburban homemaker, from file clerk to research scientist, from Olympic athlete to college president. Greater development of women's potential and fuller use of their present abilities can greatly enhance the quality of American life. We have made recommendations to this end.

We invite response to our recommendations by citizen initiative exercised in many ways—through individual inventiveness, voluntary

American Women: Report of the President's Commission on the Status of Women (Washington, D.C.: Government Printing Office, 1963).

agencies, community cooperation, commercial enterprise, corporate policy, foundation support, governmental action at various levels. In making our proposals, we have had in mind the well-being of the entire society; their adoption would in many cases be of direct benefit to men as well as women.

Certain tenets have guided our thinking. Respect for the worth and dignity of every individual and conviction that every American should have a chance to achieve the best of which he—or she—is capable are basic to the meaning of both freedom and equality in this democracy. . . .

That is why we urge changes, many of them long overdue, in the conditions of women's opportunity in the United States.

We believe that one of the greatest freedoms of the individual in a democratic society is the freedom to choose among different life patterns. Innumerable private solutions found by different individuals in search of the good life provide society with basic strength far beyond the possibilities of a dictated plan.

. . . Each woman must arrive at her contemporary expression of purpose, whether as a center of home and family, a participant in the community, a contributor to the economy, a creative artist or thinker or scientist, a citizen engaged in politics and public service. . . .

Yet there are social as well as individual determinants of freedom of choice; for example, the city slum and the poor rural crossroad frustrate natural gifts and innate human powers. It is a bitter fact that for millions of men and women economic stringency all but eliminates choice among alternatives. . . .

But while freedom of choice for many American women, as for men, is limited by economic considerations, one of the most pervasive limitations is the social climate in which women choose what they prepare themselves to do. . . .

Because too little is expected of them, many girls who graduate from high school intellectually able to do good college work do not go to college. Both they as individuals and the Nation as a society are thereby made losers.

The subtle limitations imposed by custom are . . . reinforced by specific barriers. In the course of the 20th century many bars against women that were firmly in place in 1900 have been lowered or dropped. But certain restrictions remain.

Some of these discriminatory provisions are contained in the common law. Some are written into statute. Some are upheld by court decisions. Others take the form of practices of industrial, labor, professional, or governmental organizations. . . .

Throughout its deliberations, the Commission has kept in mind certain women who have special disadvantages. Among heads of families in the United States, 1 in 10 is a woman. At least half of them are carrying responsibility for both earning the family's living and making the family's home. Their problems are correspondingly greater; their resources are usually less.

Seven million nonwhite women and girls belong to minority racial groups. Discrimination based on color is morally wrong and a source of national weakness. Such discrimination currently places an oppressive dual burden on millions of Negro women. The consultation held by the Commission on the situation of Negro women emphasized that in too many families lack of opportunity for men as well as women, linked to racial discrimination, has forced the women to assume too large a share of the family responsibility. Such women are twice as likely as other women to have to seek employment while they have preschool children at home; they are just beginning to gain entrance to the expanding fields of clerical and commercial employment; except for the few who can qualify as teachers or other professionals, they are forced into low-paid service occupations.

Hundreds of thousands of other women face somewhat similar situations: American Indians, for instance; and Spanish-Americans, many of whom live in urban centers but are new to urban life and burdened with language problems.

. . . The Commission strongly urges that in the carrying out of its recommendations, special attention be given to difficulties that are wholly or largely the products of this kind of discrimination.

The Commission has also been impressed with the extent to which lengthening life spans are causing changes in women's occupations and preoccupations from decade to decade of their adult experience. The life expectancy of a girl baby is now 73 years; it was 48 years in 1900. In comparison with her own grandmother, today's young woman has a quarter century of additional life with abundant new choices to plan for. It is essential that the counseling of girls enable them to foresee the later as well as the earlier phases of their adulthood.

. . . We were directed to review progress and make recommendations as needed for constructive action in six areas:

— Employment policies and practices, including those on wages, under Federal contracts.
— Federal social insurance and tax laws as they affect the net earnings and other income of women.

— Federal and State labor laws dealing with such matters as hours, night-work, and wages, to determine whether they are accomplishing the purposes for which they were established and whether they should be adapted to changing technological, economic, and social conditions.
— Differences in legal treatment of men and women in regard to political and civil rights, property rights, and family relations.
— New and expanded services that may be required for women as wives, mothers, and workers, including education, counseling, training, home services, and arrangements for care of children during the working day.
— The employment policies and practices of the Government of the United States with reference to additional affirmative steps which should be taken through legislation, executive, or administrative action to assure nondiscrimination on the basis of sex and to enhance constructive employment opportunities for women.

8

PAULI MURRAY

Women's Rights Are a Part of Human Rights

1964

In the late 1950s, the civil rights movement brought national attention to social injustice. The movement's foremost legislative goal was a measure to ban employment discrimination, which became Title VII of the Civil Rights Act of 1964. When a segregationist congressman from Virginia, Howard Smith, proposed an amendment to include "sex" in Title VII, many civil rights supporters balked and viewed it as a hostile amendment to defeat the legislation's passage. Women activists inside and outside

Pauli Murray, "Arguments made on behalf of including 'sex' in the employment section of the civil rights bill," contained within a letter from Pauli Murray to Marguerite Rowalt, April 14, 1964, Folder 7, Mary O. Eastwood Papers, Schlesinger Library, Radcliffe College.

Congress, however, seized the opportunity for a serious hearing on job dis-crimination against women. Pauli Murray, an African American attorney and longtime civil rights activist, had coined the phrase "Jane Crow" (a play on "Jim Crow") in the 1940s to capture the unfair treatment of all American women. While the amendment was pending, she drafted a memorandum for distribution to every member of Congress, the U.S. attorney general, and others, including Lady Bird Johnson, the president's wife.

This material has been omitted intentionally in this reprint.

This material has been omitted intentionally in this reprint.

9

NATIONAL ORGANIZATION FOR WOMEN

Statement of Purpose

1966

The fight to ensure equal employment for women spurred the creation of a new national group committed to gender justice. The National Organization for Women (NOW) became the largest mass-membership feminist organization in the country, with branches in every region and in both small towns and big cities. Members of the President's Commission on the Status of Women who were dissatisfied with lax government enforcement of the new ban on sex discrimination created NOW in June 1966 and adopted this Statement of Purpose in October. Drafted by the journalist Betty Friedan, it outlined a wide-ranging agenda for a reenergized and explicitly feminist movement that emphasized "fully equal partnership" with men in every arena of life.

We, men and women who hereby constitute ourselves as the National Organization for Women, believe that the time has come for a new

Reprinted in Betty Friedan, *It Changed My Life: Writings on the Women's Movement* (New York: Random House, 1976), 87–91.

movement toward true equality for all women in America, and toward a fully equal partnership of the sexes, as part of the world-wide revolution of human rights now taking place within and beyond our national borders.

The purpose of NOW is to take action to bring women into full participation in the mainstream of American society now, exercising all the privileges and responsibilities thereof in truly equal partnership with men.

We believe the time has come to . . . confront, with concrete action, the conditions that now prevent women from enjoying the equality of opportunity and freedom of choice which is their right as individual Americans, and as human beings.

NOW is dedicated to the proposition that women first and foremost are human beings, who, like all other people in our society, must have the chance to develop their fullest human potential. We believe that women can achieve such equality only by accepting to the full the challenges and responsibilities they share with all other people in our society, as part of the decision-making mainstream of American political, economic and social life.

We organize to initiate or support action, nationally or in any part of this nation, by individuals or organizations, to break through the silken curtain of prejudice and discrimination against women in government, industry, the professions, the churches, the political parties, the judiciary, the labor unions, in education, science, medicine, law, religion and every other field of importance in American society.

Enormous changes taking place in our society make it both possible and urgently necessary to advance the unfinished revolution of women toward true equality, now. With a life span lengthened to nearly seventy-five years, it is no longer either necessary or possible for women to devote the greater part of their lives to child rearing; yet childbearing and rearing—which continues to be a most important part of most women's lives—is still used to justify barring women from equal professional and economic participation and advance.

Today's technology . . . has virtually eliminated the quality of muscular strength as a criterion for filling most jobs, while intensifying American industry's need for creative intelligence. . . .

Despite all the talk about the status of American women in recent years, the actual position of women in the United States has declined, and is declining, to an alarming degree throughout the 1950's and 1960's. Although 46.4 percent of all American women between the ages of eighteen and sixty-five now work outside the home, the overwhelming majority—75 percent—are in routine clerical, sales, or factory jobs, or they are household workers, cleaning women, hospital attendants. About two-thirds of Negro women workers are in the lowest paid service occupations. Working women are becoming increasingly—not less—concentrated on the bottom of the job ladder. As a consequence, full-time women workers today earn on the average only 60 percent of what men earn, and that wage gap has been increasing over the past twenty-five years in every major industry group. . . .

Further, with higher education increasingly essential in today's society, too few women are entering and finishing college or going on to graduate or professional school. Today women earn only one in three of the B.A.'s and M.A.'s granted, and one in ten of the Ph.D.'s.

In all the professions considered of importance to society, and in the executive ranks of industry and government, women are losing ground. Where they are present it is only a token handful. Women comprise less than 1 percent of federal judges; less than 4 percent of all lawyers; 7 percent of doctors. Yet women represent 53 percent of the U.S. population. And increasingly men are replacing women in the top positions in secondary and elementary schools, in social work, and in libraries—once thought to be women's fields.

Official pronouncements of the advance in the status of women hide not only the reality of this dangerous decline, but the fact that nothing is being done to stop it. The excellent reports of the President's Commission on the Status of Women and of the state commissions have not been fully implemented. Such commissions . . . have no power to enforce their recommendations. . . . The reports of these commissions have, however, created a basis upon which it is now possible to build.

Discrimination in employment on the basis of sex is now prohibited by federal law, in Title VII of the Civil Rights Act of 1964. But although nearly one-third of the cases brought before the Equal Employment Opportunity Commission during the first year dealt with sex discrimination and the proportion is increasing dramatically, the commission has not made clear its intention to enforce the law with the same seriousness on behalf of women as of other victims of discrimination. Many of these cases were Negro women, who are the victims of the double discrimination of race and sex. . . .

There is no civil rights movement to speak for women, as there has been for Negroes and other victims of discrimination. The National Organization for Women must therefore begin to speak.

WE BELIEVE that the power of American law, and the protection guaranteed by the U.S. Constitution to the civil rights of all individuals, must be effectively applied and enforced to isolate and remove patterns of sex discrimination, to ensure equality of opportunity in employment and education, and equality of civil and political rights and responsibilities on behalf of women, as well as for Negroes and other deprived groups.

We realize that women's problems are linked to many broader questions of social justice; their solution will require concerted action by many groups. Therefore, convinced that human rights for all are indivisible, we expect to give active support to the common cause of equal rights for all those who suffer discrimination and deprivation, and we call upon other organizations committed to such goals to support our efforts toward equality for women. . . .

WE BELIEVE that this nation has a capacity at least as great as other nations, to innovate new social institutions which will enable women to enjoy true equality of opportunity and responsibility in society, without conflict with their responsibilities as mothers and homemakers. In such innovations, America does not lead the Western world, but lags by decades behind many European countries. We do not accept the traditional assumption that a woman has to choose between marriage and motherhood, on the one hand, and serious participation in industry or the professions on the other. . . . Above all, we reject the assumption that these problems are the unique responsibility of each individual woman, rather than a basic social dilemma which society must solve. True equality of opportunity and freedom of choice for women requires such practical and possible innovations as a nationwide network of child-care centers, which will make it unnecessary for women to retire completely from society until their children are grown, and national programs to provide retraining for women who have chosen to care for their own children full time.

WE BELIEVE that it is as essential for every girl to be educated to her full potential of human ability as it is for every boy—with the knowledge that such education is the key to effective participation in today's economy and that, for a girl as for boy, education can only be serious where there is expectation that it will be used in society. . . . We consider the decline in the proportion of women receiving higher and professional education to be evidence of discrimination. This discrimination may take the form of quotas against the admission of women to colleges and professional schools; lack of encouragement by parents, counselors and educators; denial of loans or fellowships; or the traditional or arbitrary procedures in graduate and professional training geared in terms of men, which inadvertently discriminate against women. We believe that the same serious attention must be given to high school dropouts who are girls as to boys.

WE REJECT the current assumptions that a man must carry the sole burden of supporting himself, his wife, and family, and that a woman is automatically entitled to lifelong support by a man upon her marriage, or that marriage, home and family are primarily woman's world and responsibility—hers, to dominate, his to support. We believe that a true partnership between the sexes demands a different concept of marriage, an equitable sharing of the responsibilities of home and children and of the economic burdens of their support. We believe that proper recognition should be given to the economic and social value of homemaking and child care. . . .

WE BELIEVE that women must now exercise their political rights and responsibilities as American citizens. They must refuse to be segregated on the basis of sex into separate-and-not-equal ladies' auxiliaries in the political parties, and they must demand representation according to their numbers in the regularly constituted party committees—at local, state, and national levels—and in the informal power structure, participating fully in the selection of candidates and political decision-making, and running for office themselves.

IN THE INTERESTS OF THE HUMAN DIGNITY OF WOMEN, we will protest and endeavor to change the false image of women now prevalent in the mass media, and in the texts, ceremonies, laws, and practices of our major social institutions. Such images perpetuate contempt for women by society and by women for themselves. We are similarly opposed to all policies and practices—in church, state, college, factory, or office—which, in the guise of protectiveness, not only deny opportunities but also foster in women self-denigration, dependence, and evasion of responsibility, undermine their confidence in their own abilities and foster contempt for women.

NOW WILL HOLD ITSELF INDEPENDENT OF ANY POLITICAL PARTY in order to mobilize the political power of all women and men intent on our goals. We will strive to ensure that no party, candidate, President, senator, governor, congressman, or any public official who betrays or ignores the principle of full equality between the sexes is elected or appointed to office. . . .

WE BELIEVE THAT women will do most to create a new image of women by *acting* now, and by speaking out in behalf of their own equality, freedom, and human dignity—not in pleas for special privilege, nor in enmity toward men, who are also victims of the current half-equality between the sexes—but in an active, self-respecting partnership with men. By so doing, women will develop confidence in their own ability to determine actively, in partnership with men, the conditions of their life, their choices, their future and their society.

10

KATHIE SARACHILD

A Program for Feminist "Consciousness-Raising"

1968

In the late 1960s, consciousness-raising discussions helped spread the feminist movement and build trust and community among its activists. By sharing personal stories, participants were able to reframe their experiences in collective terms and thus bring to light how gender inequality was created and reproduced. This discovery of the deeper political roots of their experiences challenged the participants to find solutions, a quest that was to generate much of the institutional innovation of women's liberation. In this document, Kathie Sarachild summarizes how the process worked.

We always stay in touch with our feelings. . . .

We assume that our feelings are telling us something from which we can learn . . . that our feelings mean something worth analyzing . . . that our feelings are saying something *political*, something reflecting fear that something bad will happen to us or hope, desire, knowledge that something good will happen to us. . . .

In our groups, let's share our feelings and pool them. Let's let ourselves go and see where our feelings lead us. Our feelings will lead us to ideas and then to actions.

First produced in 1969 and reprinted in *Notes from the Second Year: Women's Liberation* 2 (1970): 78–80.

Our feelings will lead us to our theory, our theory to our action, our feelings about that action to new theory and then to new action.

This is a consciousness-raising program for those of us who are feeling more and more that women are about the most exciting people around, at this stage of time, anyway, and that the seeds of a new and beautiful world society lie buried in the consciousness of this very class which has been abused and oppressed since the beginning of human history. It is a program planned on the assumption that a mass liberation movement will develop as more and more women begin to perceive their situation correctly and that, therefore, our primary task right now is to awaken "class" consciousness in ourselves and others on a mass scale. The following outline is just one hunch of what a theory of mass consciousness-raising would look like in skeleton form.

I. The "bitch session" cell group
   A. Ongoing consciousness expansion
      1. Personal recognition and testimony
         a. Recalling and sharing our bitter experiences
         b. Expressing our feelings about our experiences both at the time they occurred and at present
           . . .
      2. Personal testimony—methods of group practice
         a. Going around the room with key questions on key topics
         b. Speaking our experience—at random
         c. Cross examination
      3. Relating and generalizing individual testimony
           . . .
   B. Classic forms of resisting consciousness, or: How to avoid facing the awful truth
      1. Anti-womanism
      2. Glorification of the oppressor
      3. Excusing the oppressor (and feeling sorry for him)
      4. False identification with the oppressor and other socially privileged groups
      5. Shunning identification with one's own oppressed group and other oppressed groups
      6. Romantic fantasies, utopian thinking and other forms of confusing present reality with what one wishes reality to be

7. Thinking one has power in the traditional role—can "get what one wants," has power behind the throne, etc.
8. Belief that one has found an adequate personal solution or will be able to find one without large social changes
9. Self-cultivation, rugged individualism, seclusion, and other forms of go-it-alonism
10. Self-blame!!

. . .

C. Recognizing the survival reasons for resisting consciousness
D. "Starting to Stop"—overcoming repressions and delusions
   1. Daring to see, or: Taking off the rose-colored glasses
     a. Reasons for repressing one's own consciousness
       1) Fear of feeling the full weight of one's painful situation
       2) Fear of feeling one's past wasted and meaningless

       . . .

     b. Analyzing which fears are valid and which invalid
       1) Examining the objective conditions in one's own past and in the lives of most women throughout history
       2) Examining objective conditions for the present
     c. Discussing possible methods of struggle

     . . .

E. Understanding and developing radical feminist theory
   1. Using above techniques to arrive at an understanding of oppression wherever it exists in our lives. . . .
   2. Analyzing whatever privileges we may have—the white skin privilege, the education and citizenship of a big-power (imperialist) nation privilege, and seeing how these help to perpetuate our oppression as women, workers
F. Consciousness-raiser (organizer) training—so that every woman in a given bitch session cell group herself becomes an "organizer" of other groups

   . . .

II. Consciousness-raising Actions

   . . .

III. Organizing
   A. Helping new people start groups
   B. Intra-group communication and actions
     1. Monthly meetings
     2. Conferences

11

MARGARET CERULLO

Hidden History: An Illegal Abortion
1968

As feminists began to more boldly voice their concerns, issues that had never before been addressed in mass protest in the United States came to the fore and spurred wide-ranging programs for reform and cultural change. One of them was abortion, which, until 1973, was illegal in most states, although still widely practiced. Illicit abortion could be a life-threatening procedure, especially for poor women who could not afford to go to licensed doctors. In this testimony from a gathering that addressed abortion rights, Margaret Cerullo recounts her 1968 experience in a way that reveals why reproductive freedom became so important to so many.

My story is not unusual. Like many women of my generation, women now in their late thirties and forties, my commitment to abortion rights drew its initial passion from my own illegal abortion, 21 years ago. . . .

In 1968 I was 20 years old and I was a student, a junior in college at the University of Pennsylvania. . . . Against my will, and much to my dismay, I was pregnant, a fact I discovered the Saturday before my final exams were going to begin. Not only was abortion illegal in 1968, so was birth control. In Philadelphia where I lived (not a backwater) you could only get the pill (the only form of birth control I thought of) if you were married, had your parents' permission, or were 21 years of age. I was too young, I wasn't married, and my parents were practicing Catholics. . . .

I was about nine or ten weeks pregnant by the time I figured out where I could get a pregnancy test, had one, and waited for the results. I really had very little idea how I was going to go about getting an abortion, but I was absolutely clear that I did not want to have a child. Like so many young women who get pregnant, I had not been

Reprinted in Marlene Gerber Fried, ed., *From Abortion to Reproductive Freedom: Transforming a Movement* (Boston: South End Press, 1990), 87–90.

sexually active for long. I felt I was only beginning to know the possibilities of my body, as I was only beginning to dream the possibilities
of my life.

I really cannot remember exactly how I found the phone numbers,
but I suppose I got them through the various means of the underground student/political/counter-cultural scene. I began making calls
all over the East Coast, very coded telephone calls. "Hello, this is
Mary; I'm calling because I just saw John; well, actually, I saw John
about nine and a half weeks ago." You coded the relevant information
about what you wanted and how serious the situation was. I made
three or four of these calls from pay phones in between taking exams,
and the person on the other end of each one of them hung up abruptly
after I blurted out the critical information. Eventually, I found out
there was a major crackdown in process, just a chance regular kind of
repressive crackdown on illegal abortionists on the East Coast. The
weeks were ticking away and I was starting for the first time to feel
nervous. I knew after twelve weeks I would really be in trouble and I
had to go home to see my family after exams were over. I was worried
about how I would disguise nausea and morning sickness.

Finally, I got the number of the "Clergymen's [sic] Council on Problem Pregnancies" and I went to visit a clergyman in the Philadelphia
suburbs. The Council tried to match you with clergymen of your own
faith, but there were none of my faith participating. It was explained to
me that there was one place they thought it would be possible to have
an illegal abortion very quickly, a place called Towson, Maryland, outside of Baltimore. I would have to appear with $600 in small bills.

It seemed an enormous amount of money then (I was living on $5 a
week spending money) and not simple to find. (I have recently calcu-
lated that $600 in 1968 is equivalent to approximately $2,100 in 1989
dollars.) The money was what made me decide to tell the guy I had
gotten pregnant with. He agreed to dress up in a suit and go to the
bank and apply for a loan. He got it and that's how I came up with
$600 in small bills. I was to appear in Towson at 2:00 in the afternoon
outside the movie theater and wait until a man carrying a bag of groceries appeared at the theater and follow him. The clergyman with
whom I spoke suggested that I think about the experience I was going
to have as an act of civil disobedience against an unjust law. To call up
righteous anger at a moment of terror was a great help to me.

. . . I encountered the man carrying a bag of groceries. He gestured
and I went off with him to his car. There was another woman already

there, another college student. She told me later she got pregnant the first time she slept with her boyfriend. We stopped by the mall and picked up a third woman, then drove for about 45 minutes. The third woman, who was from near Towson, said that we had taken an amazingly circuitous route to arrive at a little cottage in the woods where the grocery bag man lived with his wife. . . .

The "doctor" eventually came, carrying a black bag (the sign he was a doctor) and wearing a mask that made me think of the Lone Ranger. We tossed coins to determine who would go first and proceeded to have our abortions in turn. Mine was a straightforward procedure, an old-fashioned "D&C" with no complications, and not more pain than I expected or was stoically prepared to endure. One of the other women, however, the other student, bled for a very long time, so instead of turning up back at the movie theater in Towson at 6:00 p.m. as I had been told, we didn't return until about 10:00 p.m. At about 7:00, I was allowed to call my friends in Baltimore to say I would be late, so those waiting in Towson had only about an hour and a half of anxiety that something had gone wrong or, almost unspeakable, that I would not return.

As I rode in the back seat of the car through Maryland countryside on my way to have an illegal abortion that day in May 1968, I came to a shocking realization. For the first time in my life, I understood that I was a woman, not a "human being," but a woman. For the first time, I understood something about what it meant to be a woman in this society—that the lives of women were not of value. And I realized, in an inchoate rage that is with me today as I recall this story, that in this society, *because I had sex, someone thought I deserved to die.*

12

NATIONAL ORGANIZATION FOR WOMEN

Why Feminists Want Child Care

1969

Feminists called for universally available, high-quality child care. They exposed the harm inflicted on women by a society that assigned almost all child-rearing responsibilities to mothers. This practice put women at a disadvantage in employment and political participation because they shouldered a burden that men did not. It also built unfairness into marriage, inculcated outdated gender norms in boys and girls, and deprived children of connection to their fathers. Feminist demands for government-backed quality child care built on New Deal and Great Society foundations, extending the principle of shared responsibility to the work of raising children.

A basic cause of the second-class status of women in America and the world for thousands of years has been the notion that woman's anatomy is her destiny . . . that because women bear children, it is primarily their responsibility to care for them and even that this ought to be the chief function of a mother's existence. Women will never have full opportunities to participate in our economic, political, cultural life as long as they bear this responsibility almost entirely alone and isolated from the larger world. A child socialized by one whose human role is limited, essentially, to motherhood may be proportionately deprived of varied learning experiences. In a circular fashion, the development of children has been intimately influenced by the development of women.

N.O.W. believes that the care and welfare of children is incumbent on society *and* parents. We reject the idea that mothers have a special child care role that is not to be shared equally by fathers. Men need the humanizing experiences of nurturance and guidance of another human organism.

National Organization for Women, New York Chapter, Papers, Box 10, Tamiment Library, New York University, New York, N.Y.

Developmental child care services are a right of children, parents, and the community at large, requiring immediate reallocation of national resources. In general, existing day care programs are a national disgrace in quality and availability.

Therefore, The National Organization for Women, Inc. (N.O.W.) proposes the following program for immediate implementation:

1. Comprehensive child care and development services available to all children whose families seek it.
2. High quality . . . child care programs conducive to the emotional, social, physical, and educational needs of children, subject to continual review and reassessment based on research and observation.
3. Government support of a coordinated network of developmental child care services as an immediate national priority. . . .
4. Full development of children's unique, individual potential and talents, free of sex role stereotyping, of racial, ethnic, cultural and/or economic bias, must be intrinsic orientations of child development as demonstrated by staff (women and men) behavior, educational materials and curriculum.
5. Child care services need to be available at flexible hours to meet the needs of the families who share the services.
6. Major responsibility for planning and operating the services must be a function of local control.
7. Licensing and regulatory procedures on the federal, state and local levels must be revised so they foster, rather than impede, the rapid growth of high-quality child care programs.
8. Developmental child care service is to be interpreted as including family child care, group home child care, child care centers, home visiting programs, and other innovative approaches to be developed in the future.

N.O.W. is committed to work for universally available, publicly supported, developmental child care and raising the national consciousness to public investment in this national priority. As interim steps, we support flexible fees, if any, to reflect the urgent needs and variable resources of families now.

13

ALICE DE RIVERA

On De-Segregating a High School

1969

Inspired by both the wider student movement of the 1960s and feminism, female high school students began to organize as never before. Invited to "question authority"—as a popular slogan of the time put it—young women challenged the sexism of classmates, teachers, principals, and school district officialdom. Many of their protests have been lost to the historical record, but this one by Alice de Rivera led to a lawsuit that sparked changes in New York City schools' policies. Feminists of all ages fundamentally altered education by opening math, science, shop, and sports to girls as never before in U.S. history.

Before I went to John Jay High School I hadn't realized how bad the conditions were for students. . . .

I found that students had no rights. We had no freedom of the press: many controversial articles were removed from the newspapers by the teacher-editors. We were not allowed to distribute leaflets or newspapers inside our school building, so that press communication was taken away from us. We also had no freedom of speech. . . . The school was a prison—we were required by state law to be there, but when we were there we had no rights. . . .

It was this treatment which made me as a student want to change the schools. . . .

. . . Oppression, to me, is when people are not allowed to be themselves. I encountered this condition a second time when I realized *woman's* plight in the high schools. . . .

The first time it really occurred to me that I was oppressed as a woman was when I began to think of what I was going to be when I was older. I realized I had no real plans for the future—college,

Reprinted in Robin Morgan, ed., *Sisterhood Is Powerful: An Anthology of Writings from the Women's Liberation Movement* (New York: Random House, 1970), 412–17.

maybe and after that was a dark space in my mind. In talking and listening to other girls, I found that they had either the same blank spot in their minds or were planning on marriage. If not that, they figured on taking a job of some sort *until* they got married.

The boys that I knew all had at least some slight idea in their minds of what career or job they were preparing for. Some prepared for careers in science and math by going to a specialized school. Others prepared for their later jobs as mechanics, electricians, and other tradesmen in vocational schools. . . . It seemed to me that I should fill the blank spot in my mind as the boys were able to do, and I decided to study science (biology, in particular) much more intensively. It was then that I encountered one of the many blocks which stand in the woman student's way: discrimination against women in the specialized science and math high schools in the city.

Many years before women in New York State had won their right to vote (1917), a school was established for those high-school students who wish to specialize in science and math. Naturally it was not co-ed, for women were not regarded legally or psychologically as people. This school, Stuyvesant High School, was erected in 1903. In 1956, thirty-nine years after New York women earned the right to vote, the school was renovated; yet no provision was made for girls to enter.

. . . After talking about it with my parents and friends, I decided to open up Stuyvesant and challenge the Board of Education's traditional policy.

I took my idea to Ramona Ripston, co-director of the National Emergency Civil Liberties Committee, and she accepted it warmly. Pretty soon I became involved in trying to get an application for the entrance exam to Stuyvesant filled out and sent. It was turned down and we— NECLC, my parents, and I—went to court against the principal of Stuyvesant and the Board of Ed.

The day on which we went to court was the day before the entrance exam was scheduled to be given. The Board of Ed granted me the privilege of taking the test, . . . and the judge recognized that the results of this test would be used in another court hearing to resolve whether or not I would be admitted. Five days after the other students had received their results, we found out that I had passed for entrance. . . .

We went to court again a couple of months later, in April. . . . On April 30 the New York City Board of Education voted to admit me to Stuyvesant High School in the Fall. . . .

There are a great many battles yet to be fought. . . . During my fight over Stuyvesant, I investigated the whole high-school scene, and found that out of the twenty-seven vocational high schools in the city, only *seven* are co-ed. The boys' vocational schools teach trades in electronics, plumbing, carpentry, . . . etc. The girls are taught to be beauticians, secretaries, or health aides. This means that if a girl is seeking entrance to a vocational school, she is pressured to feel that certain jobs are masculine and others feminine. She is forced to conform to the Board of Education's image of her sex. At the seven co-ed vocational schools, boys can learn clerical work, food preparation, and beauty care along with the girls. But the courses that would normally be found in a boys' school are not open to girls. . . .

. . . The argument against these schools is that "separate but equal" is not equal (as established with regard to race in the Brown Decision). The psychological result of the school which is segregated by sex—only because of tradition—is to impress upon girls that they are only "flighty females" who would bother the boys' study habits (as a consequence of girls not being interested in anything but the male sex). This insinuates immaturity on the part of girls—and certainly produces it in both sexes. A boy who has never worked with a girl in the classroom is bound to think of her as his intellectual inferior, and will not treat her as if she had any capacity for understanding things other than child care and homemaking. Both sexes learn to deal with each other as non-people. It really messes up the growth of a person's mind.

Out of the sixty-two high schools in New York City, twenty-nine are now sexually segregated. I believe that it is up to the girls to put pressure on the Board of Education to change this situation. . . .

All girls have been brought up by this society never being able to be themselves—the school system has reinforced this. My desire at this time is to change the educational situation to benefit *all* the students. . . . So, since I don't want *my* issues to get swallowed up in the supposed "larger" issues, I'm going to make women's liberation the center of my fight.

14

THE FEMINISTS

Women: Do You Know the Facts about Marriage?

1969

Women's liberationists were appalled at the mounting evidence of gender bias in every aspect of American life. One measure of women's inferior standing was marital law, which privileged men to the point of making a husband's rape of his wife legal in most states. This 1969 leaflet exposes the facts of New York law, but it also illustrates how feminists could be arrogant toward women who didn't "get it." Handed out at a demonstration against the city Marriage License Bureau, the leaflet takes an in-your-face approach to criticizing marriage. Bold actions like this created publicity for women's liberation, but also caused problems when women who valued conventional families reacted against feminism.

Women: Do You Know the Facts about Marriage?

DO YOU KNOW THAT RAPE IS LEGAL IN MARRIAGE?

According to law, *sex* is the purpose of marriage. You have to have sexual intercourse in order to have a valid marriage.

DO YOU KNOW THAT LOVE AND AFFECTION ARE NOT REQUIRED IN MARRIAGE?

If you can't have sex with your husband, he can get a divorce or annulment. If he doesn't love you, that's *not* grounds for divorce.

DO YOU KNOW THAT YOU ARE YOUR HUSBAND'S PRISONER?

You have to live with him wherever *he* pleases. If he decides to move someplace else, either you go with him or he can charge you with desertion, get a divorce and, according to law, you deserve nothing because *you're the guilty party.* And that's if *he* were the one who moved!

Reprinted in Robin Morgan ed., *Sisterhood Is Powerful: An Anthology of Writings from the Women's Liberation Movement* (New York: Vintage Books, 1970), 601–2.

DO YOU KNOW THAT, ACCORDING TO THE UNITED NATIONS, MARRIAGE
IS A "SLAVERY-LIKE PRACTICE"?

According to the marriage contract, your husband is entitled to more
household services from you than he would be from a live-in maid. So,
why aren't you getting paid? Under law, you're entitled only to "bed
and board."

When you got married, did you know these facts? If you didn't know,
what did you *think* you were consenting to? But these are the *laws*. If
you *had* known the terms, would you have signed the contract?

Do You Resent This Fraud?

All the discriminatory practices against women are patterned and
rationalized by this slavery-like practice. We can't destroy the inequities
between men and women until we destroy marriage. *We must free ourselves. And marriage is the place to begin.*

15

GAINESVILLE WOMEN'S LIBERATION

What Men Can Do for Women's Liberation

1970

*Feminists held different views about whether and how men could help their
cause. The National Organization for Women purposely took the name
"for Women" rather than "of Women" to emphasize that they considered
equality for women a political and not a biological commitment and welcomed men as members. Self-described "radical feminists," in contrast,
embraced separatism as a positive good, not just a strategy for developing
confidence and power. All women's liberation activists wanted autonomous
women-only organizations. Taking their cue from Black Power advocates,*

Reprinted in Rosalyn Baxandall and Linda Gordon, eds., *Dear Sisters: Dispatches from
the Women's Liberation Movement* (New York: Basic Books, 2000), 76–77.

who told whites to fight racism among other whites, women's liberationists urged men to concentrate on changing men's attitudes and reforming the institutions they dominated. Some men took their advice and contributed to cultural changes by challenging sexism where they found it.

At the center of the Women's Liberation Movement is a demand that men change the way they have been acting towards women for centuries. Because of its central importance to the movement, the Women's Liberation groups in Gainesville focused on the question "What can men do now for women's liberation?" and agreed on the following answers. . . .

- Set up a day-care center at the shop or place of work so that more women can be free to work.
- Exercise no job discrimination toward women at any level (whether this be done officially or personally).
- Refuse to work where women aren't given equal pay and let the employer know how you feel about it.
- Have as much confidence in a woman doctor as you would a man. If she's a woman and has made it, you can be sure that she is qualified.
- Encourage other men to do what has been considered "women's work" in the past.
- If your wife wants to keep her own name or doesn't want to wear a wedding band, view this not as a rejection, but as an indication of her desire to enter into a fully adult and equal relationship. She is with you by choice, not compulsion.
- If you can't cook, learn.
- Share in all the housework without being asked, not just the occasional jobs like painting the kitchen or fixing a leaky pipe.
- You helped conceive the children, so share in their upbringing. That includes babysitting, diaper-changing, feeding, dressing, and everything on an equal basis with your wife.
- Fathers should provide a model for their children that is not male supremacist. Break with standard house-keeping patterns. Encourage children of both sexes to help equally with chores when it's chore time. Don't laugh at boys if they show an interest in cooking or washing dishes (many do) or little girls if they want to learn to build things.

— Don't buy your son educational toys and your daughter a doll.
— Push your high school to make home economics and industrial arts compulsory for boys and girls. Boys need cooking
  skills as much as girls need mechanical know-how.
— Push your school principals and guidance counselors to allow
  girls to attend high school while pregnant and afterwards.
— Stop punishing girls who don't play dumb.
— Don't say one thing among your men friends and another to a
  woman. A woman cannot correct you or challenge the inaccu-
  racies of your thinking if she doesn't know what it is you
  really *are* thinking. And even though it is not easy to challenge all the ideas that your male friends have held and bene-
  fited from for centuries, it is a necessity in changing the ideas
  of the whole society.
— Don't descend to man talk in which women are talked about
  as if they were animals. "My chick," "I screwed the pig," etc.
  Insist that other men stop talking this way.
— Listen to a woman's ideas. Hers are as good as a man's or
  better.
— Don't ask a woman to pay for everything with sex.
— Stop being patronizing. See a woman for what she is. Don't
  trap her and yourself by acting like she's beneath you.
— Provide babysitting and transportation for WL meetings.
— Don't say you believe in women's liberation and then take
  advantage of a woman. Don't use women's liberation as a
  weapon to get out of doing things or to take liberties.
  ("You're liberated now, so you can carry your own groceries."
  "You're an equal now, so I can hit you.")
— Don't be super critical of a woman's behavior because she is
  in Women's Liberation. Don't expect her to act like a liberated woman until you become a liberated man.
— Don't try and make points with women by bragging what a
  non–male supremacist you are. Admit your chauvinism so we
  can try and help you get out of it.
— Don't make jokes about WL. It's a serious thing. Women die
  from male supremacy every year.

16

YOUNG LORDS PARTY

Position Paper on Women

1970

Women organized for equality not only in feminist groups but in other progressive movements as well. The Young Lords was a New York–based Puerto Rican liberation organization, with politics similar to the Black Panther Party. When Young Lords women challenged the largely male leadership to take a stand on sexism, the group issued this position paper. Notable here also is the criticism of forcible sterilization of Puerto Rican women and the defense of their right to children.

Puerto Rican, Black, and other Third World (colonized) women are becoming more aware of their oppression in the past and today. They are suffering three different types of oppression under capitalism. First, they are oppressed as Puerto Ricans or Blacks. Second, they are oppressed as women. Third, they are oppressed by their own men.

In the past women were oppressed by several institutions, one of which was marriage. In Latin America and Puerto Rico, the man had a wife and another woman, called *la corteja*. This condition still exists today. The wife was there to be a homemaker, to have children and to maintain the family name and honor. She had to be sure to be a virgin and remain pure for the rest of their life, meaning she could never experience sexual pleasure. The wife had to have children in order to enhance the man's concept of virility and his position within the Puerto Rican society. *La corteja* became his sexual instrument. The man could have set her up in another household, paid her rent, bought her food, and paid her bills. He could have children with this woman. Both women had to be loyal to the men. Both sets of children grew up very confused and insecure.

Women have always been expected to be wives and mothers only. They are respected by the rest of the community for being good

Reprinted in Rosalyn Baxandall and Linda Gordon, eds., *Dear Sisters: Dispatches from the Women's Liberation Movement* (New York: Basic Books, 2000), 38–40.

cooks, good housewives, good mothers, but never for being intelligent, strong, educated or militant. In the past, women were not educated, only the sons got an education and mothers were respected for the number of sons they had, not daughters. Daughters were worthless and the only thing they could do was marry early to get away from home. At home the role of the daughter was to be a nursemaid for the other children and kitchen help for her mother.

The daughter was guarded like a hawk by her father, brothers and uncles to keep her a virgin. In Latin America the people used *dueñas* or old lady watchdogs to guard the purity of the daughters. The husband must be sure that his new wife has never been touched by another man because that would ruin the "merchandise." . . .

Sex was a subject that was never discussed, and women were brainwashed into believing that the sex act was dirty and immoral, and its only function was for the making of children.

Puerto Rican and Black men are looked upon as rough, athletic and sexual, but not as intellectuals. Puerto Rican women are not expected to know anything except about the home, kitchen and bedroom. All that they are expected to do is look pretty and add a little humor. The Puerto Rican man sees himself as superior to his women, and his superiority, he feels, gives him license to do many things—curse, drink, use drugs, beat women and run around with many women. As a matter of fact these things are considered natural for a man to do and he must do them to be considered a man. A woman who curses, drinks and runs around with a lot of men is considered dirty scum, crazy, and a whore.

Today, Puerto Rican men are involved in a political movement. Yet the majority of their women are home taking care of the children. The Puerto Rican sister that involves herself is considered aggressive, castrating, hard and unwomanly, viewed by the brothers as sexually accessible because what is she doing outside of the home? . . .

Machismo has always been a very basic part of Latin American and Puerto Rican culture. Machismo is male chauvinism and more. He can do whatever he wants because his woman is an object with certain already defined roles—wife, mother and good woman.

Machismo means physical abuse, punishment and torture. A Puerto Rican man will beat his woman to keep her in place and show her who's boss. Most Puerto Rican men do not beat women publicly because in the eyes of other men that is a weak thing to do. So they usually wait until they're home. All the anger and violence of centuries of oppression which should be directed against the oppressor is directed at the Puerto Rican woman. The aggression is also directed at daughters. The daughters hear their fathers saying "the only way a woman is going to do anything or listen is by hitting her." The father applies this to the daughter, beating her so that she can learn *respeto*. The daughters grow up with messed-up attitudes about their role as women and about manhood. They grow to expect that men will always beat them. . . .

Third World sisters are caught up in a complex situation. On one hand, we feel that genocide is being committed against our people. We know that Puerto Ricans will not be around on the face of the earth very long if Puerto Rican women are sterilized at the rate they are being sterilized now. The practice of sterilization in Puerto Rico goes back to the 1930s when doctors pushed it as the only means of contraception. In 1947–48, 7% of the women were sterilized; between 1953 and 1954, 4 out of every 25; and by 1956 the number had increased to about 1 out of 3 women. In many cases our sisters are told that their tubes are going to be "tied" but are never told that the "tying" is really "cutting" and that the tubes can never be "untied."

Part of this genocide is also the use of birth control pills which were tested for 15 years on Puerto Rican sisters before being sold on the market in the U.S. Even now many doctors feel that these pills cause cancer and death from blood clotting.

Abortions in hospitals that are butcher shops are little better than the illegal abortions our women used to get. The first abortion death in NYC under the new abortion law was Carmen Rodriguez, a Puerto Rican sister who died in Lincoln Hospital. Her abortion was legal but the conditions in the hospital were deadly.

On the other hand, we believe that abortions should be legal if they are community controlled, if they are safe, if our people are educated about the risks and if doctors do not sterilize our sisters while performing abortions. We realize that under capitalism our sisters and brothers cannot support large families and the more children we have the harder it is to support them. We say: change the system so that women can freely be allowed to have as many children as they want without suffering. . . .

17

PAT MAINARDI

The Politics of Housework

1970

Women's liberationists developed insightful analyses of the subtle work-ings of male power in everyday life, often with humorous exposés that boosted women's confidence to seek change while deftly parrying men's resistance. Deemed a job for women alone, housework left women with the "double day" after work or school, while their husbands or boyfriends enjoyed leisure time. Pat Mainardi made the topic fun, but her bite is unmistakable. Her manifesto evokes to the many household struggles it took to change gender expectations and create equitable intimate rela-tionships between men and women.

Liberated women—very different from women's liberation! The first signals all kinds of goodies, to warm the hearts (not to mention other parts) of the most radical men. The other signals—*housework*. The first brings sex without marriage, sex before marriage, cozy house-keeping arrangements ("You see, I'm living with this chick") and the self-content of knowing that you're not the kind of man who wants a doormat instead of a woman. . . .

On the other hand is women's liberation—and housework. What? You say this is all trivial? Wonderful! That's what I thought. It seemed perfectly reasonable. We both had careers, both had to work a couple of days a week to earn enough to live on, so why shouldn't we share the housework? So I suggested it to my mate and he agreed—most men are too hip to turn you down flat. "You're right," he said, "It's only fair."

Then an interesting thing happened. I can only explain it by stating that we women have been brainwashed more than even we can imag-ine. Probably too many years of seeing television women in ecstasy over their shiny waxed floors or breaking down over their dirty shirt

Reprinted in Robin Morgan, ed., *Sisterhood Is Powerful: An Anthology of Writings from the Women's Liberation Movement* (New York: Vintage Books, 1970), 501–10.

collars. Men have no such conditioning. They recognize the essential fact of housework right from the very beginning. Which is that it stinks. Here's my list of dirty chores: buying groceries, carting them home and putting them away; cooking meals and washing dishes and pots; doing the laundry, digging out the place when things get out of control; washing floors. The list could go on but the sheer necessities are bad enough. All of us have to do these things, or get someone else to do them for us. The longer my husband contemplated these chores the more repulsed he became, and so proceeded the change from the normally sweet considerate Dr. Jekyll into the crafty Mr. Hyde who would stop at nothing to avoid the horrors of—*housework*. . . . Housework trivial? Not on your life! Just try to share the burden.

So ensued a dialogue that's been going on for several years. Here are some of the high points:

"I don't mind sharing the housework, but I don't do it very well. We should each do the things we're best at."
Meaning: Unfortunately I'm no good at things like washing dishes or cooking. What I do best is a little light carpentry, changing light bulbs, moving furniture (*how often do you move furniture?*).
Also Meaning: Historically the lower classes (black men and us) have had hundreds of years experience doing menial jobs. It would be a waste of manpower to train someone else to do them now.
Also Meaning: I don't like the dull stupid boring jobs, so you should do them.

"I don't mind sharing the work, but you'll have to show me how to do it."
Meaning: I ask a lot of questions and you'll have to show me everything everytime I do it because I don't remember so good. Also don't try to sit down and read while I'm doing my jobs because I'm going to annoy hell out of you until it's easier to do them yourself.

"We used to be so happy!" (Said whenever it was his turn to do something.)
Meaning: I used to be so happy.
Meaning: Life without housework is bliss. (*No quarrel here. Perfect agreement.*)

"We have different standards, and why should I have to work to your standards. That's unfair."

Meaning: If I begin to get bugged by the dirt and crap I will say "This place sure is a sty" or "How can anyone live like this?" and wait for your reaction. I know that all women have a sore called "Guilt over a messy house." . . . I can outwait you.

Also Meaning: I can provoke innumerable scenes over the housework issue. Eventually doing all the housework yourself will be less painful to you than trying to get me to do half. Or I'll suggest we get a maid. She will do my share of the work. You will do yours. It's women's work.

"I've got nothing against sharing the housework, but you can't make me do it on your schedule."

Meaning: Passive resistance. I'll do it when I damned well please, if at all. If my job is doing dishes, it's easier to do them once a week. If taking out laundry, once a month. If washing the floors, once a year. If you don't like it, do it yourself oftener, and then I won't do it at all.

"I *hate* it more than you. You don't mind it so much."

Meaning: Housework is garbage work. It's the worst crap I've ever done. It's degrading and humiliating for someone of *my* intelligence to do it. But for someone of *your* intelligence . . .

"Housework is too trivial to even talk about."

Meaning: It's even more trivial to do. Housework is beneath my status. My purpose in life is to deal with matters of significance. . . . You should do the housework.

"Women's liberation isn't really a political movement."

Meaning: The Revolution is coming too close to home.

18

A WOMEN'S HEALTH COLLECTIVE

The Male-Feasance of Health

1970

Many women worked in the health care industry and nearly all dealt with the system as consumers. From consciousness-raising discussions, some feminists realized the ways in which contemporary medicine was harmful to women. Among the issues they brought to light were the unsafe amounts of hormones in some birth control pills, the pervasive abuse of sterilization, and the unnecessary use of hysterectomies. This critique, written by a women's health group and published in an underground newspaper, revealed how the pursuit of profit and the sexist attitudes rife among male doctors hurt female patients and workers. Although the egalitarian vision of this document was never realized, feminists achieved many successes by pushing for patients' and workers' rights and better information and accountability.

The American health care system is a disaster for almost everyone who tries to use it. All consumers face continually escalating prices for services which are increasingly fragmented, depersonalized and just plain hard to find. All health workers face a rigid, doctor-dominated hierarchy, where all but the top jobs are low-paid dead-ends. But certain groups are especially oppressed by the American health system, both as workers and as consumers. Black and brown people suffer not only because they are poor but because of the built-in racism of most medical institutions. Less appreciated, but potentially just as explosive, is the specific oppression of women—of all classes and races—by the health system.

To start with, women are much more dependent on the health system than are men. Women consume the bulk of America's health services: they make, on the average, 25 percent more visits to the doctor per year than men, and more than 100 percent more if mothers' visits to take their children to the doctor are counted. Women consume

Rat: Subterranean News (March 7–21, 1970): 9.

50 percent more prescription drugs than men, and are admitted to hospitals much more frequently than men. As workers, women have always depended on the health system as one of the few places where a woman could always find a job. About 70 percent of all health workers, and 75 percent of all hospital workers, are women. Thus whatever goes wrong with the health system is a problem, by and large, for women.

As in almost every other institution of American life, however, it is men—doctors, medical school deans, hospital directors and trustees, and drug and insurance company executives—who make the decisions. Men decide which jobs will be available to women health workers, how much they will be paid and even what kind of uniform they will wear. For women health consumers, men decide on the most personal issues of health care—what form of birth control a woman should use, whether she should have an abortion, what method of childbirth she should use, and of course, how much she should be told about the risks and options. In their exercise of power over women, men in medicine are no more objective and scientific than any other men. They start with an irrational image of women as ignorant and passive dependents of men, and they reinforce that image in every aspect of the health system. . . .

For women health workers, this means being type-cast into jobs which are subordinate and subservient to men. Throughout the health system, men occupy the scientifically interesting, or authoritative, positions; women do the scut work. Women, not men, are nurses, not because women are more "nurse-like" than men, but because from grade school on, women are encouraged to aim no higher than nursing. Women are not encouraged to take science courses in high school and college, and they are actively discouraged from entering medical school. Nursing itself is supposed to be a specifically feminine occupation, requiring no initiative or ability to reason. And as one medical school dean put it, "The reason that nurses are all women is that men couldn't put up with the kind of relationship that a nurse has to doctors." The doctor-nurse relationship is always authoritarian, and often characterized by subtle or overt sexual manipulation of the nurse-handmaid. . . .

Women as health consumers are oppressed by the same male supremacist attitudes and institutionalized practices which oppress women as health workers. When they enter a hospital or a doctor's office, women encounter a hierarchy dominated by men, in which they see women playing only subservient roles. . . . Women are assumed to be emotional and "difficult," so they are often classified as "neurotic" well before physical illness has been ruled out. . . . And women are assumed to be vain, so they are the special prey of the paramedical dieting, cosmetics, and plastic surgery businesses.

. . . The institutional and attitudinal sources of oppression are the same for both women workers and consumers. Already there are the first signs of an alliance between women workers and consumers—an alliance which will shake the male-dominated health system to its foundations.

19

SUSAN GRIFFIN

Rape Is a Form of Mass Terrorism
1970

Forcible sex is one way that men can exert power over women and dominance over other men. For thousands of years, in warfare and slavery, the rape of the opponents' women followed and signified conquest. For centuries, legal codes treated rape as a crime against a father's or husband's "property" and honor, not as an offense against the woman herself. By this logic, rape in marriage was perfectly legal. Women's consciousness-raising discussions led to a sophisticated understanding that spurred the formation of rape crisis centers and organizing for legal and law enforcement changes.

Rape is an act of aggression in which the victim is denied her self-determination. It is an act of violence which, if not actually followed by beatings or murder, nevertheless always carries with it the threat of death. And finally, rape is a form of mass terrorism, for the victims of rape are chosen indiscriminately, but the propagandists for male supremacy broadcast that it is women who cause rape by being unchaste or in the wrong place at the wrong time—in essence, by behaving as though they were free.

The threat of rape is used to deny women employment. (In California, the Berkeley Public Library, until pushed by the Federal Employment

Ramparts 10, no. 3 (September 1971): 26–35.

Practices Commission, refused to hire female shelvers because of perverted men in the stacks.) The fear of rape keeps women off the streets at night. Keeps women at home. Keeps women passive and modest for fear that they be thought provocative.

It is part of human dignity to be able to defend oneself, and women are learning. Some women have learned karate; some to shoot guns. And yet we will not be free until the threat of rape and the atmosphere of violence is ended, and to end that the nature of male behavior must change.

But rape is not an isolated act that can be rooted out from patriarchy without ending patriarchy itself. The same men and power structure who victimize women are engaged in the act of raping Vietnam, raping black people and the very earth we live upon. Rape is a classic act of domination where, in the words of Kate Millett, "the emotions of hatred, contempt, and the desire to break or violate personality," takes place. This breaking of the personality characterizes modern life itself. No simple reforms can eliminate rape. As the symbolic expression of the white male hierarchy, rape is the quintessential act of our civilization, one which, Valerie Solanis warns, is in danger of "humping itself to death."

20

RADICALESBIANS

The Woman-Identified Woman

1970

Lesbians had long been active in the women's movement, but when they spoke up about lesbian concerns in the late 1960s, they encountered homophobia from heterosexual feminists, most publicly from NOW leader Betty Friedan. In response, a new group called the Radicalesbians issued this manifesto for a new kind of politics: lesbian feminism. They declared that lesbians, as totally "women-identified women," were the true feminist radicals.

Reprinted in Karla Jay and Allen Young, eds., *Out of the Closets: Voices of Gay Liberation* (New York: Douglas Book Corp., 1972), 172–77.

What is a lesbian? A lesbian is the rage of all women condensed to the point of explosion. She is the woman who, often beginning at an extremely early age, acts in accordance with her inner compulsion to be a more complete and freer human being than her society . . . cares to allow her. These needs and actions, over a period of years, bring her into painful conflict with people, situations, the accepted ways of thinking, feeling and behaving, until she is in a state of continual war with everything around her, and usually with her self. She may not be fully conscious of the political implications of what for her began as personal necessity, but on some level she has not been able to accept the limitations and oppression laid on her by the most basic role of her society—the female role. The turmoil she experiences tends to induce guilt proportional to the degree to which she feels she is not meeting social expectations. . . . To the extent that she cannot expel the heavy socialization that goes with being female, she can never truly find peace with herself. . . .

It should first be understood that lesbianism, like male homosexuality, is a category of behavior possible only in a sexist society characterized by rigid sex roles and dominated by male supremacy. Those sex roles dehumanize women by defining us as a supportive/serving caste *in relation to* the master caste of men, and emotionally cripple men by demanding that they be alienated from their own bodies and emotions in order to perform their economic/political/military functions effectively. Homosexuality is a by-product of a particular way of setting up roles (or approved patterns of behavior) on the basis of sex; as such it is an inauthentic (not consonant with "reality") category. In a society in which men do not oppress women, and sexual expression is allowed to follow feelings, the categories of homosexuality and heterosexuality would disappear.

But lesbianism is also different from male homosexuality, and serves a different function in the society. "Dyke" is a different kind of put-down from "faggot," although both imply you are not playing your socially assigned sex role—are not therefore a "real woman" or a "real man." The grudging admiration felt for the tomboy and the queasiness felt around a sissy boy point to the same thing: the contempt in which women—or those who play a female role—are held. And the investment in keeping women in that contemptuous role is very great. Lesbian is the word, the label, the condition that holds women in line. When a woman hears this word tossed her way, she knows she is stepping out of line. She knows that she has crossed the terrible boundary of her sex role. She recoils, she protests, she reshapes her

actions to gain approval. Lesbian is a label invented by the man to
throw at any woman who dares to be his equal, who dares to challenge his prerogatives, . . . who dares to assert the primacy of her own
needs. To have the label applied to people active in women's liberation
is just the most recent instance of a long history; older women will
recall that not so long ago, any woman who was successful, independent, not orienting her whole life about a man, would hear this word.
For in this sexist society, for a woman to be independent means she
can't be a *woman*—she *must* be a *dyke*. . . . When you strip off all the
packaging, you must finally realize that the essence of being a
"woman" is to get fucked by men. . . .

Women in the movement have in most cases gone to great lengths
to avoid discussion and confrontation with the issue of lesbianism. It
puts people up-tight. They are hostile, evasive, or try to incorporate it
into some "broader issue." They would rather not talk about it. If they
have to, they try to dismiss it as a "lavender herring." But it is no side
issue. It is absolutely essential to the success and fulfillment of the
women's liberation movement that this issue be dealt with. As long as
the label "dyke" can be used to frighten women into a less militant
stand, keep her separate from her sisters, keep her from giving primacy to anything other than men and family—then to that extent she
is controlled by the male culture. Until women see in each other the
possibility of a primal commitment which includes sexual love, they will
be denying themselves the love and value they readily accord to men,
thus affirming their second-class status. As long as male acceptability is
primary . . . the term lesbian will be used effectively against women. . . .
And the most crucial aspect of the acceptability is to deny lesbianism—
i.e., deny any fundamental challenge to the basis of the female role. . . .

. . . Some younger, more radical women have honestly begun to discuss lesbianism, but so far it has been primarily as a sexual "alternative" to men. This, however, is still giving primacy to men, both
because the idea of relating more completely to women occurs as a
negative reaction to men, and because the lesbian relationship is being
characterized simply by sex. . . . What is crucial is that women begin
disengaging from male-defined response patterns. . . .

But why is it that women have related to and through men? By
virtue of having been brought up in a male society, we have internalized the male culture's definition of ourselves. That definition views us
as relative beings who exist not for ourselves, but for the servicing,
maintenance and comfort of men. That definition consigns us to sexual and family functions, and excludes us from defining and shaping

the terms of our lives. In exchange for our psychic servicing and for performing society's non-profit-making functions, the man confers on us just one thing: the slave status which makes us legitimate in the eyes of the society in which we live. This is called "femininity" or "being a real woman" in our cultural lingo. We are authentic, legitimate, real to the extent that we are the property of some man whose name we bear. To be a woman who belongs to no man is to be invisible, pathetic, inauthentic, unreal. . . . As long as we are dependent on the male culture for this definition, for this approval, we cannot be free.

The consequence of internalizing this role is an enormous reservoir of self-hate. This is not to say the self-hate is recognized or accepted as such; indeed most women would deny it. It may be experienced as discomfort with her role, as feeling empty, as numbness, as restlessness, a paralyzing anxiety at the center. Alternatively, it may be expressed in shrill defensiveness of the glory and destiny of her role. But it does exist, often beneath the edge of her consciousness, poisoning her existence, keeping her alienated from herself, her own needs, and rendering her a stranger to other women. . . . Women resist relating on all levels to other women who will reflect their own oppression, their own secondary status, their own self-hate. For to confront another woman is finally to confront one's self—the self we have gone to such lengths to avoid. And in that mirror we know we cannot really respect and love that which we have been made to be.

As the source of self-hate and the lack of real self are rooted in our male-given identity, we must create a new sense of self. As long as we cling to the idea of "being a woman," we will sense some conflict with that incipient self, that sense of I, that sense of a whole person. It is very difficult to realize and accept that being "feminine" and being a whole person are irreconcilable. Only women can give each other a new sense of self. That identity we have to develop with reference to ourselves, and not in relation to men. This consciousness is the revolutionary force from which all else will follow. . . . For this we must be available and supportive to one another . . . give the emotional support necessary to sustain this movement. Our energies must flow toward our sisters, not backwards towards our oppressors. . . .

. . . With that real self, with that consciousness, we begin a revolution to end the imposition of all coercive identifications, and to achieve maximum autonomy in human expression.

21

FIRST NATIONAL CHICANA CONFERENCE

Workshop Resolutions

1971

In the early days of the new feminist activism, many expected that gender would be the great unifier, bringing together women from all walks of life. Those most likely to proclaim universal sisterhood were white, middle-class women who assumed their experiences and values were universal. Minority women, however, challenged their concepts of gender. In 1971, at the First National Chicana Conference, La Conferencia de Mujeres por la Raza, *in Houston, Texas, six hundred young Mexican American women discussed their experiences and stated their concerns. The resolutions that came from the conference are notable for being sex-positive among a group that was subjected to conservative Catholic teachings about sex, Anglo complaints about high Chicana birth rates, and exploitative reproductive-control experiments.*

Sex and the Chicana

We feel that in order to provide an effective measure to correct the many sexual hangups facing the Chicano community the following resolutions should be implemented:

I. Sex is good and healthy for both Chicanos and Chicanas and we must develop this attitude.

II. We should destroy the myth that religion and culture control our sexual lives.

III. We recognize that we have been oppressed by religion and that the religious writing was done by *men* and interpreted by *men*. Therefore, for those who desire religion, they should interpret their Bible or Catholic rulings according to their own feelings, what they think is right, without any guilt complexes.

Reprinted in Mirta Vidal, ed., *Chicanas Speak Out* (New York: Pathfinder Press, 1971), 13–15, and in Rosalyn Baxandall and Linda Gordon, eds., *Dear Sisters: Dispatches from the Women's Liberation Movement* (New York: Basic Books, 2000), 166.

IV. Mothers should teach their sons to respect women as human beings who are equal in every respect. *No double standard.*

V. Women should go back to the communities and form discussion and action groups concerning sex education.

VI. Free, legal abortions and birth control for the Chicano community, controlled by *Chicanas.* As Chicanas we have the right to control our own bodies.

VII. Make use of church centers, neighborhood centers and any other place available. . . .

Chicanas should understand that Chicanos face oppression and discrimination, but this does not mean that the Chicana should be a scapegoat for the man's frustrations.

With involvement in the movement, marriages must change. Traditional roles for Chicanas are not acceptable or applicable.

RESOLUTIONS:

I. We, as *mujeres de La Raza*, recognize the Catholic Church as an oppressive institution and do hereby resolve to break away and not go to it to bless our unions.

II. Whereas: Unwanted pregnancies are the basis of many social problems, and

Whereas: The role of Mexican American women has traditionally been limited to the home, and

Whereas: The need for self-determination and the right to govern their own bodies is a necessity for the freedom of all people, therefore,

BE IT RESOLVED: That the National Chicana Conference go on record as supporting free family planning and free and legal abortions for all women who want or need them.

III. Whereas: Due to socio-economic and cultural conditions, Chicanas are often heads of households, i.e., widows, divorcees, unwed mothers, or deserted mothers, or must work to supplement family income, and

Whereas: Chicana motherhood should not preclude educational, political, social, and economic advancement, and

Whereas: There is a critical need for a 24-hour child-care center in Chicano communities, therefore,

BE IT RESOLVED: That the National Chicana Conference go on record as recommending that every Chicano community promote and set up 24-hour day-care facilities, and that it be further resolved that these facilities will reflect the concept of La Raza as the united family, and on the basis of brotherhood (La Raza), so that men, women, young and old assume the responsibility for the love, care, education, and orientation of all the children of Aztlán.

IV. Whereas: Dr. Goldzieher of SWRF has conducted an experiment on Chicana women of westside San Antonio, Texas, using a new birth control drug, and

Whereas: No human being should be used for experimental purposes, therefore,

BE IT RESOLVED: That this Conference send telegrams to the American Medical Association condemning this act.

22

JOHNNIE TILLMON

Welfare Is a Women's Issue

1972

The radical ferment of the 1960s encouraged even the most vulnerable Americans to organize, among them poor mothers who relied on public assistance to raise their children. Founded in 1966, the National Welfare Rights Organization (NWRO) used direct-action protest to win decent incomes from the federal safety net program called Aid to Families with Dependent Children (AFDC). NWRO also fought the agency's intrusion into the personal lives of welfare recipients, such as midnight raids to see if any men who might be able to support them resided in the house. As welfare rights activists resisted the degrading aspects of AFDC, they developed an explicitly feminist politics, as this piece illustrates.

I'm a woman. I'm a black woman. I'm a poor woman. I'm a fat woman. I'm a middle-aged woman. And I'm on welfare.

In this country, if you're any one of those things—poor, black, fat, female, middle-aged, on welfare—you count less as a human being. If you're all those things, you don't count at all. Except as a statistic.

Liberation News Service 415 (February 26, 1972): 15–16. Reprinted in Rosalyn Baxandall, Linda Gordon, and Susan Reverby, eds., *America's Working Women: A Documentary History* (New York: Vintage Books, 1976).

I am a statistic.

I am 45 years old. I have raised six children.

I grew up in Arkansas, and I worked there for fifteen years in a laundry, making about $20 or $30 a week, picking cotton on the side for carfare. I moved to California in 1959 and worked in a laundry there for nearly four years. In 1963 I got too sick to work anymore. Friends helped me to go on welfare.

They didn't call it welfare. They called it A.F.D.C.—Aid to Families with Dependent Children. Each month I get $363 for my kids and me. I pay $128 a month rent; $30 for utilities, which include gas, electricity, and water; $120 for food and non-edible household essentials; $50 for school lunches for the three children in junior and senior high school who are not eligible for reduced-cost meal programs.

There are millions of statistics like me. Some on welfare. Some not. And some, really poor, who don't even know they're entitled to welfare. Not all of them are black. Not at all. In fact, the majority—about two-thirds—of all the poor families in the country are white.

Welfare's like a traffic accident. It can happen to anybody, but especially it happens to women.

And that is why welfare is a women's issue. For a lot of middle-class women in this country, Women's Liberation is a matter of concern. For women on welfare it's a matter of survival.

Forty-four percent of all poor families are headed by women. That's bad enough. But the *families* on A.F.D.C. aren't really families. Because 99 percent of them are headed by women. That means there is no man around. In half the states there really can't be men around because A.F.D.C. says if there is an "able-bodied" man around, then you can't be on welfare. If the kids are going to eat, and the man can't get a job, then he's got to go. So his kids can eat.

The truth is that A.F.D.C. is like a supersexist marriage. You trade in *a* man for *the* man. But you can't divorce him if he treats you bad. He can divorce you, of course, cut you off anytime he wants. But in that case, *he* keeps the kids, not you.

The man runs everything. In ordinary marriage, sex is supposed to be for your husband. On A.F.D.C. you're not supposed to have any sex at all. You give up control of your own body. It's a condition of aid. You may even have to agree to get your tubes tied so you can never have more children just to avoid being cut off welfare.

The man, the welfare system, controls your money. He tells you what to buy, what not to buy, where to buy it, and how much things cost. If things—rent, for instance—really cost more than he says they do, it's just too bad for you.

There are other welfare programs, other kinds of people on welfare—the blind, the disabled, the aged. (Many of them are women, too, especially the aged.) Those others make up just over a third of all the welfare caseloads. We A.F.D.C.s are two-thirds.

But when the politicians talk about the "welfare cancer eating at our vitals," they're not talking about the aged, blind, and disabled. Nobody minds them. They're the "deserving poor." Politicians are talking about A.F.D.C. Politicians are talking about us—the women who head up 99 percent of the A.F.D.C. families—and our kids. We're the "cancer," the "undeserving poor." Mothers and children.

In this country we believe in something called the "work ethic." That means that your work is what gives you human worth. But the work ethic itself is a double standard. It applies to men and to women on welfare. It doesn't apply to all women. If you're a society lady from Scarsdale and you spend all your time sitting on your prosperity paring your nails, well, that's okay.

The truth is a job doesn't necessarily mean an adequate income. A woman with three kids—not twelve kids, mind you, just three kids—that woman earning the full federal minimum wage of $2.00 an hour, is still stuck in poverty. She is below the government's own official poverty line. There are some ten million jobs that now pay less than the minimum wage, and if you're a woman, you've got the best chance of getting one.

... There is no dignity in starvation. Nobody denies, least of all poor women, that there is dignity and satisfaction in being able to support your kids through honest labor.

We wish we could do it.

The problem is that our country's economic policies deny the dignity and satisfaction of self-sufficiency to millions of people—the millions who suffer everyday in underpaid dirty jobs—and still don't have enough to survive.

People still believe that old lie that A.F.D.C. mothers keep on having kids just to get a bigger welfare check. On the average, another baby means another $35 a month—barely enough for food and clothing. Having babies for profit is a lie that only men could make up, and only men could believe. Men, who never have to bear the babies or have to raise them and maybe send them to war.

There are a lot of other lies that male society tells about welfare mothers; that A.F.D.C. mothers are immoral, that A.F.D.C. mothers are lazy, misuse their welfare checks, spend it all on booze and are stupid and incompetent.

If people are willing to believe these lies, it's partly because they're just special versions of the lies that society tells about *all* women.

For instance, the notion that all A.F.D.C. mothers are lazy: that's just a negative version of the idea that women don't work and don't want to. It's a way of rationalizing the male policy of keeping women as domestic slaves.

The notion that A.F.D.C. mothers are immoral is another way of saying that all women are likely to become whores unless they're kept under control by men and marriage. Even many of my own sisters on welfare believe these things about themselves.

On TV, a woman learns that human worth means beauty and that beauty means being thin, white, young and rich.

She learns that her body is really disgusting the way it is, and that she needs all kinds of expensive cosmetics to cover it up.

She learns that a "real woman" spends her time worrying about how her bathroom bowl smells; that being important means being middle class, having two cars, a house in the suburbs, and a minidress under your maxicoat. In other words, an A.F.D.C. mother learns that being a "real woman" means being all the things she isn't and having all the things she can't have.

Either it breaks you, and you start hating yourself, or you break it.

There's one good thing about welfare. It kills your illusions about yourself, and about where this society is really at. It's laid out for you straight. You have to learn to fight, to be aggressive, or you just don't make it. If you can survive being on welfare, you can survive anything. . . .

Maybe it is we poor welfare women who will really liberate women in this country. We've already started on our welfare plan.

Along with other welfare recipients, we have organized together so we can have some voice. Our group is called the National Welfare Rights Organization (N.W.R.O.). We put together our own welfare plan, called Guaranteed Adequate Income (G.A.I.), which would eliminate sexism from welfare.

There would be no "categories"—men, women, children, single, married, kids, no kids—just poor people who need aid. You'd get paid according to need and family size only—$6,500 for a family of four (which is the Department of Labor's estimate of what's adequate), and that would be upped as the cost of living goes up.

If I were president, I would solve this so-called welfare crisis in a minute and go a long way toward liberating every woman. I'd just issue a proclamation that "women's" work is *real* work.

In other words, I'd start paying women a living wage for doing the work we are already doing—child-raising and housekeeping. And the welfare crisis would be over, just like that. Housewives would be getting wages, too—a legally determined percentage of their husband's salary—instead of having to ask for and account for money they've already earned.

For me, Women's Liberation is simple. No woman in this country can feel dignified, no woman can be liberated, until all women get off their knees. That's what N.W.R.O. is all about—women standing together, on their feet.

23

CHICAGO WOMEN'S LIBERATION UNION

Socialist Feminism: A Strategy for the Women's Movement

1972

One of the most influential currents in women's liberation was socialist feminism. Its advocates revealed how capitalism and male dominance combined to the detriment of women and how gender, class, and race intermingled to shape experience, consciousness, and politics. This document from a Chicago group shows how they linked women's liberation to a more egalitarian, democratic, and humane society.

We choose to identify ourselves with the heritage and future of feminism and socialism in our struggle for revolution.

From feminism we have come to understand an institutionalized system of oppression based on the domination of men over women: sexism. . . .

Hyde Park Chapter, Chicago Women's Liberation Union, *Socialist Feminism: A Strategy for the Women's Movement* (Chicago: Chicago Women's Liberation Union, 1972). Reprinted in Rosalyn Baxandall and Linda Gordon, eds., *Dear Sisters: Dispatches from the Women's Liberation Movement* (New York: Basic Books, 2000), 96–100.

But we share a particular conception of feminism that is socialist. It is one that focuses on how power has been denied women because of their class position. We see capitalism as an institutionalized form of oppression based on profit for private owners of publicly-worked-for wealth. It sets into motion hostile social relations in classes. . . .

We share the socialist vision of a humanist world made possible through a redistribution of wealth and an end to the distinction between the ruling class and those who are ruled.

The following would be *among* the things we envision in the new order, part of everyday life for all people:

— Free, humane, competent medical care with an emphasis on preventive medicine, under the service of community organizations

— People's control over their own bodies—i.e., access to safe, free birth control, abortion, sterilization, free from coercion or social stigma

— Attractive, comfortable housing designed to allow for private and collective living

— Varied, nutritious, abundant diet

— Social respect for the work people do, understanding that all jobs can be made socially necessary and important

— Democratic councils through which all people control the decisions which most directly affect their lives on the job, in the home, and community

— Scientific resources geared toward the improvement of life for all, rather than conquest and destruction through military and police aggression

— Varied, quality consumer products to meet our needs

— An end of housework as private, unpaid labor

— Redefinition of jobs, with adequate training to prepare people for jobs of their choice; rotation of jobs to meet the life cycle needs of those working at them, as well as those receiving the services

— Political and civil liberties which would encourage the participation of all people in the political life of the country

— Disarming of and community control of police

— Social responsibility for the raising of children and free client-controlled childcare available on a 24-hour basis to accommodate the needs of those who use it and work in it

— Free, public quality education integrated with work and community activities for people of all ages
— Freedom to define social and sexual relationships
— A popular culture which enhances rather than degrades one's self-respect and respect for others
— Support for internal development and self-determination for countries around the world

We find it futile to argue which is more primary—capitalism or sexism. We are oppressed by both. As they are systems united against our interests, so our struggle is against both. This understanding implies more than women's caucuses in a "movement" organization. What we as socialist feminists need are organizations which can work for our particular vision, our self-interest in a way that will guarantee the combined fight against sexism and capitalism. At times this will mean independent organizations, at other times joint activity. . . .

THE PROJECT SHOULD:

— be broken into parts and fought as reforms that can conceivably be won
— provide step-by-step activity for involvement

Here is an example of how some of us developed one project— fighting for child care with the Action Committee for Decent Childcare.

We had decided that a struggle for free, 24-hour, client-controlled childcare would meet our ideological criteria. . . .

We spent three months gathering information about every aspect of the issue of childcare and considering all of the alternatives for vying for power. After the initial period, research was used to serve actions. We immediately eliminated the federal level since it is too remote to attack without a national organization to force some change. However, in instances where local offices really have power they might be appropriate targets. State and local agencies (and perhaps a few federal branches with responsibility for implementing guidelines or overseeing state and local programs) appeared to be easier and more successful targets. With the state level dominated by Republicans and the local level by Democrats (as is often the case) we also considered ways to play one off against the other. . . .

After examining each of the above areas with the continual question of what we could do to meet women's real needs, give women a sense of their power and alter power relations, we decided on an initial strategy. Given the funding situation, we focused on licensing, an equally great problem, but one that was more manageable. Existing licensing laws prevented centers from opening rather than encouraging new centers.

Women became involved because of their need for childcare. Day care operators joined because we could provide services, communication and expose their problems with the city government in order to win real changes. This meant they took risks of retaliation by the city (any center can be closed down by using the arbitrary licensing laws against them) until enough operators were involved and singling out any one individual became difficult. Those who were vulnerable had parents organized for protection (with community hearings, tours for the press of beautiful centers about to be closed down for lack of political pull).

Although initially we believed our constituency would be all white (this was our base in the beginning), we very successfully developed a black and white organization on the basis of self-interest. In a black area, women demanded the creation of childcare centers, because there were none. In an adjoining white area, women demanded that the few existing centers not be closed down. Once united, other common issues were raised. . . .

24

PHYLLIS SCHLAFLY

What's Wrong with "Equal Rights" for Women?

1972

Phyllis Schlafly, a St. Louis attorney and mother of six, was a conservative activist for two decades before her fight to defeat the Equal Rights Amendment (ERA). In this document from her STOP ERA campaign, Schlafly appealed to homemakers who feared feminism. In a society where

The Phyllis Schlafly Report 5, no. 7 (February 1972): 1–4.

losing her husband could condemn a woman and her children to poverty,
Schlafly's followers came to agree that equality was dangerous.

Of all the classes of people who ever lived, the American woman is the most privileged. We have the most rights and rewards, and the fewest duties. Our unique status is the result of a fortunate combination of circumstances.

1. We have the immense good fortune to live in a civilization which respects the family as the basic unit of society. This respect is part and parcel of our laws and our customs. It is based on the fact of life—which no legislation or agitation can erase—that women have babies and men don't.

If you don't like this fundamental difference, you will have to take up your complaint with God because He created us this way. The fact that women, not men, have babies is not the fault of selfish and domineering men, or of the establishment, or of any clique of conspirators who want to oppress women. It's simply the way God made us.

Our Judeo-Christian civilization has developed the law and custom that, since women must bear the physical consequences of the sex act, men must be required to bear the *other* consequences and pay in other ways. These laws and customs decree that a man must carry his share by physical protection and financial support of his children and of the woman who bears his children, and also by a code of behavior which benefits and protects both the woman and the children.

The Greatest Achievement of Women's Rights

This is accomplished by the institution of the family. . . . It assures a woman the most precious and important right of all—the right to keep her own baby and to be supported and protected in the enjoyment of watching her baby grow and develop.

The institution of the family is advantageous for women for many reasons. After all, what do we want out of life? To love and be loved? Mankind has not discovered a better nest for a lifetime of reciprocal love. A sense of achievement? A man may search 30 to 40 years for accomplishment in his profession. A woman can enjoy real achievement when she is young—by having a baby. She can have the satisfaction of doing a job well—and being recognized for it.

Do we want financial security? We are fortunate to have the great legacy of Moses, the Ten Commandments, especially this one: "Honor thy father and thy mother that thy days may be long upon the land." Children are a woman's best social security—her best guarantee of social benefits such as old age pension, unemployment compensation, workman's compensation, and sick leave. The family gives a woman the physical, financial and emotional security of the home—for all her life.

The Financial Benefits of Chivalry

2. The second reason why American women are a privileged group is that we are the beneficiaries of a tradition of special respect for women which dates from the Christian Age of Chivalry. The honor and respect paid to Mary, the Mother of Christ, resulted in all women, in effect, being put on a pedestal. . . .

In other civilizations, such as the African and the American Indian, the men strut around wearing feathers and beads and hunting and fishing (great sport for men!), while the women do all the hard, tiresome drudgery including the tilling of the soil (if any is done), the hewing of wood, the making of fires, the carrying of water, as well as the cooking, sewing and caring for babies.

This is not the American way because we were lucky enough to inherit the traditions of the Age of Chivalry. In America, a man's first significant purchase is a diamond for his bride, and the largest financial investment of his life is a home for her to live in. . . .

The Real Liberation of Women

3. The third reason why American women are so well off is that the great American free enterprise system has produced remarkable inventors who have lifted the backbreaking "women's work" from our shoulders.

In other countries and in other eras, it was truly said that "Man may work from sun to sun, but woman's work is never done." Other women have labored every waking hour—preparing food on wood-burning stoves, making flour, baking bread in stone ovens, spinning yarn, making clothes, making soap, doing the laundry by hand, heating irons, making candles for light and fires for warmth, and trying to nurse their babies through illnesses without medical care.

The real liberation of women from the backbreaking drudgery of centuries is the American free enterprise system which stimulated inventive geniuses to pursue their talents—and we all reap the profits. The great heroes of women's liberation are not the straggly-haired

women on television talk shows and picket lines, but Thomas Edison
who brought the miracle of electricity to our homes to give light and
to run all those labor-saving devices. . . .

The Fraud of the Equal Rights Amendment

In the last couple of years, a noisy movement has sprung up agitating
for "women's rights." Suddenly, everywhere we are afflicted with
aggressive females on television talk shows yapping about how mis-
treated American women are, suggesting that marriage has put us in
some kind of "slavery," that housework is menial and degrading,
and—perish the thought—that women are discriminated against.
New "women's liberation" organizations are popping up . . . and pur-
porting to speak for some 100,000,000 American women.

It's time to set the record straight. The claim that American women
are downtrodden and unfairly treated is the fraud of the century. The
truth is that American women never had it so good. Why should we
lower ourselves to "equal rights" when we already have the status of
special privilege?

The proposed Equal Rights Amendment states: "Equality of rights
under the law shall not be denied or abridged by the United States or
by any state on account of sex." So what's wrong with that? Well, here
are a few examples of what's wrong with it.

This Amendment will absolutely and positively make women subject
to the draft. . . . Foxholes are bad enough for men, but they certainly
are *not* the place for women—and we should reject any proposal
which would put them there in the name of "equal rights." . . .

Another bad effect of the Equal Rights Amendment is that it will
abolish a woman's right to child support and alimony, and substitute
what the women's libbers think is a more "equal" policy, that "such
decisions should be within the discretion of the Court and should be
made on the economic situation and need of the parties in the case."

Under present American laws, the man is *always* required to support
his wife and each child he caused to be brought into the world. Why
should women abandon these good laws—by trading them for something so nebulous and uncertain as the "discretion of the Court"? . . .

By law and custom in America, in case of divorce, the mother
always is given custody of her children unless there is overwhelming
evidence of mistreatment, neglect or bad character. This is our special
privilege because of the high rank that is placed on motherhood in our
society. Do women really want to give up this special privilege and
lower themselves to "equal rights" . . . ? I think not.

Women's Libbers Do NOT Speak for Us

The "women's lib" movement is *not* an honest effort to secure better jobs for women who want or need to work outside the home. This is just the superficial sweet-talk to win broad support for a radical "movement." Women's lib is a total assault on the role of the American woman as wife and mother, and on the family as the basic unit of society.

Women's libbers are trying to make wives and mothers unhappy with their career, make them feel that they are "second-class citizens" and "abject slaves." Women's libbers are promoting free sex instead of the "slavery" of marriage. They are promoting Federal "day-care centers" for babies instead of homes. They are promoting abortions instead of families. . . .

If the women's libbers want to reject marriage and motherhood, it's a free country and that is their choice. But let's not permit these women's libbers to get away with pretending to speak for the rest of us. Let's not permit this tiny minority to degrade the role that most women prefer. Let's not let these women's libbers deprive wives and mothers of the rights we now possess.

Tell your Senators NOW that you want them to vote NO on the Equal Rights Amendment. Tell your television and radio stations that you want equal time to present the case FOR marriage and motherhood.

25

SUSAN JACOBY

Feminism in the $12,000-a-Year Family
1973

The mainstream media sensationalized feminism, with the focus usually on young, attractive women or women who could be stereotyped as manhaters. This created problems of accountability in the movement because those interviewed were often not serious organizers. It also led to

Susan Jacoby, "What Do I Do for the Next 20 Years?" *New York Times Magazine* (June 17, 1973): 10–11, 39–43, 49. Reprinted in Rosalyn Baxandall, Linda Gordon, and Susan Reverby, eds., *America's Working Women: A Documentary History* (New York: Vintage Books, 1976), 384–89.

portrayals that failed to capture the movement's actual diversity. Still, the coverage moved many women to a new awareness, including older house- wives who would not dream of attending a feminist meeting but took up the phrase "male chauvinist pig" to criticize sexist men. Issues of class and aging are examined in this account of an informal consciousness- raising group among Italian and Jewish women married to men in blue- collar and white-collar jobs.

The life stories outlined by these women have many common elements. The women are all in their 40's; most grew up in first- and second- generation Italian or Jewish immigrant homes. A few have lived in East Flatbush since they were children and the rest came from nearby blue-collar neighborhoods. Most of the women graduated from high school, went to work for a year or two at poorly paid jobs, married by age 20 and quickly started having children. Only two of the 12 had any education beyond high school. Rose Danielli's background is typical; she worked as a telephone operator for a year before marrying Joe, a telephone installer, when they were both 19.

The husbands are blue-collar union men or white-collar workers employed by the city government; their general income range is between $9,000 and $14,000 a year. Most of the families have at least three children. Homemade soups and clothes are a necessary econ- omy for them rather than an expression of the "traditional female role." Their houses represent the only important financial investment of their lives and are maintained with appropriate care—postage-stamp lawns raked free of leaves, living-room sofas glazed with plastic slip- covers and reserved for company, starched kitchen curtains, home freezers stocked with the specials the women unearth in numerous grocery stores on Saturday mornings. . . .

Whatever their problems, the women love their husbands and are not about to leave them. They do not expect to liberate themselves by living alone, although they understand why some younger women find marriage an unsatisfactory state. They have neither the education nor the work experience to be tapped as token women for high-powered jobs in high-powered companies. . . .

Nevertheless, the women are convinced that they can build a future different from the traditional path laid out by their mothers and grand- mothers. The feminist movement is responsible in large measure for their belief that they can change the course of their middle-aged lives.

The movement was gaining strength and national publicity at a time when the women who make up the East Flatbush group began to face the void most full-time mothers experience after their children grow up and leave home. Their comments in the group sessions indicate that two main concerns spurred their interest in feminism: the feeling that society in general, and their husbands in particular, no longer viewed them as sexually interesting or even sexually functioning women, and the realization that they were "out of a job" in the same sense as a middle-aged man who is fired by his employer of 20 years. . . .

The most important decision at the first meeting was that the sessions would be held regularly on Tuesday nights. Except in emergencies, they would not be subject to interference by children and husbands who had other activities in mind. At the second session, several women reported with glee that the announcement of a regular meeting had caused a storm in their homes. "In our house, my husband expects me home every evening," explained one woman. "That is, unless he decides to go bowling. Then I can go to the movies by myself or out to a neighbor's."

Some of the husbands resented the decision to regularize the meetings because they had chosen to view the group as just another coffee klatsch. The reactions of the men included bitter opposition, secret sabotage, amused resignation and quiet support. "My poor man asked what he should tell the neighbors if they called and asked for me on Tuesday night," recalled a woman whose husband is part-owner of a Jewish delicatessen. "I told him to tell anyone who called the truth, that I'm working out what to do with my life. He said the hell he would, he'd tell them I was doing something for the temple." . . .

"Life plays a dirty trick on women," said Ann Nussbaum, whose husband is a bookkeeper with the city Finance Administration. "The men think you're gorgeous when you're too young to know anything about life. How well I remember how hard it was to take any interest in my husband when I had been changing diapers all day. Now I have much more time and interest for sex, but my husband is the one who's beat. He does tax returns to make extra money on the side — I know he just feels like rolling over and going to sleep at the end of the day.

"One of the things I feel I have to get across to him is that being physically affectionate with each other doesn't have to mean sex; he doesn't have to feel all this pressure that men seem to feel about performance. I agree with Ruth that it's hard to talk about these things after a lifetime of being silent, but I don't see how we can get anywhere unless we speak up about what's bothering us." . . .

Ruth Levine, who had never worked outside her home, surprised the rest of the group by becoming the first to take the plunge into the job market. She applied for a job as a file clerk in a large advertising agency and was hired with a warning from the personnel department that "most of the girls on your floor will be 25 years younger than you are." . . .

"Well, I know it's not much of a job in the eyes of anyone else," she reported to her group after she had been working for a month. "Even the secretaries look down on file clerks—especially a file clerk in her 40's. And I agree with some of the stuff I read in *Ms.* these days—a man, even a dumb one, would never have to take one of these jobs. But to me the job is something. . . . What do I get out of the job? For one thing, I get to meet a lot of different people who give me new things to think about. . . ."

The other important thing Ruth gets out of her job is money: She brings home more than $90 a week after taxes and Social Security withholding. "It makes me feel both that I'm independent and that I'm contributing something to the household," she said. . . .

Ruth is taking a shorthand course so that she can move into a better-paying secretarial job next fall. After she took the first step, four other women in the group found jobs. Two returned to the secretarial work they had done before they were married, one found an opening as a teacher aide in the Head Start program for preschool children, and another put her fluent Italian to work as an interpreter for older immigrants in their dealing with city agencies. Two women in the group decided they would go to college and were accepted in adult-education programs leading toward a bachelor's degree. The women who plan to enter college are undergoing profound changes that have also made a deep impact on their husbands. . . .

In general, the East Flatbush men who disapprove of feminism express their reactions more openly than the professional husbands of upper-middle-class women who are the most vocal and visible participants in the movement. College-educated men are often reluctant to attack women's liberation in principle, but their practical behavior is another matter. Judging from the wide variety of male reactions described by the Flatbush wives, Middle-American men are no more or no less disturbed than other American men when the women in their lives try to break out of the traditional female pattern.

The East Flatbush women have considerable difficulty identifying with the widely publicized leaders of the movement. Said one: "I confess I don't feel much of a sense of sisterhood when I see pictures of Gloria Steinem with her streaked hair and slinky figure. I feel somehow that these people don't know how it is to be getting older with very little money and education. They have it a lot better than we do—it's not true that we're all in the same boat."

Another woman disagreed: "Well, there's one thing that we all have in common—we're all afraid of muggers and rapists when we walk down a dark street at night. And that's something we have in common with the colored women who live right here in East Flatbush, even though most of us are better off financially than they are."

The women do identify with the movement on a variety of specific issues—child day-care centers, equal pay for equal work, the right to abortion and contraceptive information, the need to educate young girls to think of themselves as individuals in their own right instead of viewing themselves only as future wives and mothers. Several of the women now spend considerable time trying to introduce these re-formist ideas into the conservative environment of East Flatbush. One of their immediate goals is a health information service for girls and women of all ages; they feel that most East Flatbush women are unlikely to use the referral services now available in Manhatten. Rose Danielli had hoped to organize such a service through her church but ran head-on into a clash with her priest over contraceptive information.

"My husband said, 'Oh, Rose, don't get into a battle with Father ———.' Then he said, 'I give up. If you were willing to do battle with my mama you won't stop with the priest.'"

26

MARGARET SLOAN

Black Feminism: A New Mandate

1974

Among women of color, African Americans were the most vocal in exposing the limitations of white women's analyses and programs. Black feminists, whose activist traditions gave them unique authority, contributed disproportionately to the movement's development. Believing that the civil rights movement did not pay enough attention to gender and sexism

Ms. (May 1974): 99ff.

and that the feminist movement did not pay enough attention to race and racism, a group of African American women formed the National Black Feminist Organization in 1973. Meeting in the offices of New York NOW, thirty women launched the new organization in May, held a press conference in August, and organized a national convention in November.

Much of the time, at the New York offices of the National Black Feminist Organization, the phone calls and visitors are enthusiastic and supportive. Others are tentative and curious. Some are questioning, a few suspicious. But since NBFO surfaced last year with a press conference in August and a highly successful Eastern Regional Conference in November, the phone hasn't stopped ringing, the mailbags bulge, and the monthly meetings are full of new faces.

This sort of response from all over the country has proved that, for many black women, the timing was right. But others—from the media, the black community, and even some in the Women's Movement— seem confused, if not threatened. So NBFO spends quite a lot of time carefully defining itself and its goals. "Standard Questions You Might Be Asked . . . Suggested Answers That Might Work"—a series of exchanges that have the ring of experience—is an essential part of the organizing package for new members:

Q: Are you not separating from the Black Movement and thereby dividing the black race?
A: No, not at all. Black women comprise over half of the black population in this country. We see ourselves as strengthening the black community by calling upon all the talents of an entire people to combat racism. We feel that there can't be liberation for less than half a race. We want *all* black people in this country to be free, and by organizing around our needs as black women, we are making sure that we won't be left out. . . . It is very difficult to get anyone to work on issues that are not close to their experience. Welfare, domestic workers, reproductive freedom, the unwed mother, and many other areas are issues we feel are not being adequately addressed. A host of other issues— the professional black woman, sexuality, unemployment—also affect us as black women.

Q. Are you part of the Women's Liberation Movement?
A. Very much so. Many of us come out of the Women's Movement, and are still active in a variety of its organizations, but we felt that the

duality of being black and female made us want to organize around those things which affect us most. It is very important that we, as black women, set our own priorities. We will lend support to feminist organizations and will work in coalitions that affect the 53 percent majority—the women in this country.

Notes on One Day in May

The moment was a Sunday in May. About 30 of us sat in closeness because the room was not big enough. We had known about this day for a long time and had made plans, well in advance, to be there. It was the day that would change our lives . . . and we knew it. . . .

It was a busy three hours. We all had so much to say. Our relationship with the feminist movement, our participation in the Black Movement. We listened. We laughed. We interrupted each other, not out of disrespect, but out of that immediate identification with those words and feelings that we had each said and felt . . . many times alone. We had all felt crazy and guilty about our beliefs. And yet, all the things that have divided black women from each other in the past, kept us from getting to that room sooner, seemed not to be important. . . .

We were excited, but at the same time a certain calmness rested on our words. We knew that we were creating our own "herstory," and we had never been in a situation where there were so many black women who understood feminism. . . .

July and August

Much antifeminist media coverage on black women. "Women's Lib has no soul," says one black magazine. National newsweekly has negative article written by a white woman. Black male leader says that the Supreme Court decision making abortion legal for all women means genocide for black people. Everybody is speaking for the black woman. We have to speak out. Press conference . . . announce ourselves as a National Black Feminist Organization. . . .

August 17

A lot of reporters came to the press conference. Phone has not stopped ringing. "What took you so long, sisters?" "How can I join?" We were right all along. What are we going to do with these names?

Must have meeting while the momentum is high. Meeting one week
later was attended by 200 black women. . . .

November Conference

More than 500 black women. Not just East Coast—California, Mississippi, Chicago, Seattle. . . .

At Present

1,000 women on our mailing list and several "unofficial" chapters. We
are in that inevitable internal growth process. We are learning from
each other and growing beyond our mistakes. Maybe one day there
will be a chapter in every state . . . every city . . . a dream? Well, so was
NBFO.

27

LETHA SCANZONI

For the Christian, the Idea of Human Freedom Shouldn't Be Threatening

1976

*As the movement surged, women from varied faiths developed a feminist
consciousness and sought to change their denominations, with liberal
Jews and Christians leading the way. The first female Reform rabbi
achieved ordination in 1972, and the Episcopal Church recognized the
ordination of fifteen women in 1976. Fundamentalist and Catholic
women faced a much bigger challenge, but even in conservative religious
traditions, women and some men began to reexamine the Bible and to
question church teachings. This letter from the evangelical feminist
leader and author Letha Scanzoni to a husband who was unnerved by
his wife's quest for equality reveals evangelical feminists' challenges and
the resources that sustained them.*

Letha Scanzoni, "How to Live with a Liberated Wife," *Christianity Today* 20, no. 18 (June 4,
1976): 6–9.

Dear Doug,

I was glad to get your letter. You needn't apologize for feeling bewildered about what has been happening in Jan's life and in your marriage since she became involved in the women's movement. . . . Having talked to other Christian husbands, I can assure you you're not alone.

Many men share that sense of *uneasiness* ("What's happening to us? What does it all mean? What changes will have to take place?"), *hurt* ("I tried my best to make her happy. Isn't what I have to offer her enough?"), *resentment* ("Why can't life go on as it always has? My wife used to seem perfectly content."), even *fear* ("Maybe she'll get so independent she won't need me anymore! Maybe she'll even get ideas about leaving! Or maybe women will take over things, and we men will lose our masculinity."). . . .

For the Christian, the idea of human freedom shouldn't be threatening. Jesus described his mission in terms of freedom, saying he was sent "to set at liberty those who are oppressed" (Luke 4:18). True, we can spiritualize that, or at least limit it, and say he came to free us from sin, guilt, the fear of death, and the bondage of the law—and simply let it go at that. But mind-boggling as such great theological truths are, I'm convinced there's even more to the freedom Christ grants. He said he came that we might experience life in all its abundance, and I think an important part of abundant life is living up to one's potential—being able to fulfill the Creator's design for oneself. If gender-role stereotypes keep a person from using his or her God-given gifts when they don't happen to fit into some preconceived notion of what is "proper" for one's sex, we ought to work to remove them.

When you ask me what women want today, the answer is simple: we want to be free to live up to our *full human potential*. You want to be free to live up to your potential, and Jan is asking the same for herself. It's what she meant in saying that she is only now beginning to see herself as a complete person in her own right and not simply as an extension of you—as "Jan" rather than as "Mrs. Doug."

I think you can understand that. Think how you would feel if you were told that you could experience life outside the home only in a vicarious, second-hand way, that the big world was something in which you didn't really have a part except as you experienced it and influenced it through the activities of someone very close to you. Chances are you'd wonder why you couldn't participate directly instead of living a kind of life-once-removed. . . .

We are bold to say: "God created me a woman, and I rejoice in that. I know that God made both male and female in his image and charged both sexes with the responsibility of having dominion over the earth.

That means I'm responsible for using the abilities and talents God gave me, and there's no reason to limit the kind of service I can give to the world simply because I was born female."

Why have I gone into all this? Because you said you sincerely want to understand what your wife has been going through as she rethinks who she is and what she should do with her life. This matter of choice or life options (rather than having a certain role imposed from the outside for no other reason than that one was born of a certain race or sex) is at the heart of the questioning large numbers of people are doing today. And right along with that questioning is an awakening to a sense of responsibility (we might call it stewardship in the case of the Christian) for developing and using talents to the full. . . .

For some women, full-time homemaking is career enough — at least at certain stages of life. And they should never be made to feel guilty for wanting to spend those years in child-rearing and making the home happy and comfortable for the whole family. . . .

However, for other women, full-time homemaking doesn't use their particular talents to the full. Why should they be made to feel guilty about that? Why shouldn't they be encouraged to put their talents to work where they can *best* be used? All of us would be better off — the Church, the society, the women themselves, and yes, their husbands and children. Wanting to develop oneself fully and use talents shouldn't be equated with selfishness. The person who feels fulfilled as a human being — man or woman — is going to have much more to offer others than he or she would have if blocked from that fulfillment.

"But why can't all women be fulfilled simply by being wives and mothers?" you ask. Let's try a variation of that question. "Why can't all men be fulfilled simply by being husbands and fathers?" I think you'd say those are fine, exciting roles, but that there are other areas of life where a man wants to make contributions as well — not "instead of" but "in addition to." . . .

The question is this: How willing are you as a Christian husband to give up time and energy by sharing in household tasks and child-care so that Jan won't be forced to carry a double load when she starts her college courses? . . .

Do all you can to show her you feel it's your responsibility as much as hers to care for the kids and house. You're *sharing* a life, both in the home and in what you each bring to the home from outside, whether in the form of money you've earned, or ideas you've learned, or new friends, contacts, books, and magazines you bring in based on your interests. You're not "helping her" with "her" work—you're sharing together.

... Think of the love depicted in First Corinthians 13. Patience. Kindness. Putting away irritability and resentment (even in the midst of the adjustments and increased flexibility required of the family). Dealing with jealousy (some men feel threatened because their wives find meaning and identity in activities outside the home, and some male egos seem too fragile to bear competence on the part of women). Not insisting on one's own way (even if one has been used to having it as an assumed male right in the past). These are some messages from First Corinthians 13 that seem on target for husbands who want to show love in the midst of the changes many wives are asking. . . .

Actually, you have a marvelous adventure ahead of you as you and Jan work out this new life together. Studies have shown that the more gender-segregated the roles of husband and wife are, the more a couple's world is divided into "men's work and interests" and "women's work and interests," the less satisfactory is the marital relationship in the areas of companionship, leisure interests, and physical affection. As women and men have more educational and career interests in common, they're likely to have an enhanced sense of loving partnership, and every area of marriage can be enriched because two fulfilled persons are bringing much more to their relationship.

Jan has a lot to offer the world, Doug. Yet her steps toward using her God-given talents are likely to be hesitant without your wholehearted support. I know how much my husband's support has meant in my life. . . . John looked for, encouraged, and "stirred up" gifts in me that I didn't even know were there!

You can do that for your wife, too. As you do, her love for you will grow, and so will yours for her, as you see her develop her potential and know you've been an important part of that development. . . . Believe me, this kind of marriage never gets boring because both partners are always learning and growing and have so much to exchange with each other. God bless you both.

YOUR SISTER IN CHRIST,
Letha

28

Letter from a Battered Wife

ca. 1976

Prior to the women's movement, wife-beating was unlikely to result in criminal prosecution or other public-policy redress. Police treated battery as a "private" matter between a husband and wife, and women who were beaten had nowhere to turn for help. Feminists who worked with battered women and studied the problem learned that it was not an anomaly but a very common syndrome rooted in the historical power granted to men in marriage and perpetuated by women's relative social powerlessness. Del Martin's book Battered Wives, *from which this letter is taken, created a better understanding of brutality toward women in intimate relationships and helped generate new support for victims of domestic violence. Del Martin was a founder of the Daughters of Bilitis. Her work on wife-beating offers an example of how lesbians advanced feminist thought and practice.*

I am in my thirties and so is my husband. I have a high school diploma and am presently attending a local college, trying to obtain the additional education I need. My husband is a college graduate and a professional in his field. We are both attractive and, for the most part, respected and well-liked. We have four children and live in a middle-class home with all the comforts we could possibly want.

I have everything, except life without fear.

For most of my married life I have been periodically beaten by my husband. What do I mean by "beaten"? I mean that parts of my body have been hit violently and repeatedly, and that painful bruises, swelling, bleeding wounds, unconsciousness, and combinations of these things have resulted.

Beating should be distinguished from all other kinds of physical abuse—including being hit and shoved around. When I say my husband threatens me with abuse I do not mean he warns me that he may

Del Martin, *Battered Wives* (San Francisco: Glide Publications, 1976), 1–4.

lose control. I mean that he shakes a fist against my face or nose, makes punching-bag jabs at my shoulder, or makes similar gestures which may quickly turn into a full-fledged beating.

I have had glasses thrown at me. I have been kicked in the abdomen when I was visibly pregnant. I have been kicked off the bed and hit while lying on the floor—again, while I was pregnant. I have been whipped, kicked and thrown, picked up again and thrown down again. I have been punched and kicked in the head, chest, face, and abdomen more times than I can count.

I have been slapped for saying something about politics, for having a different view about religion, for swearing, for crying, for wanting to have intercourse.

I have been threatened when I wouldn't do something he told me to do. I have been threatened when he's had a bad day and when he's had a good day.

I have been threatened, slapped, and beaten after stating bitterly that I didn't like what he was doing with another woman.

After each beating my husband has left the house and remained away for days.

Few people have ever seen my black and blue face or swollen lips because I have always stayed indoors afterwards, feeling ashamed. I was never able to drive following one of these beatings, so I could not get myself to a hospital for care. I could never have left my young children alone, even if I could have driven a car.

Hysteria inevitably sets in after a beating. This hysteria—the shaking and crying and mumbling—is not accepted by anyone, so there has never been anyone to call.

My husband on a few occasions did phone a day or so later so we could agree on the excuse I would use for returning to work, the grocery store, the dentist appointment, and so on. I used the excuses—a car accident, oral surgery, things like that.

Now, the first response to this story, which I myself think of, will be "Why didn't you seek help?"

I did. Early in our marriage I went to a clergyman who, after a few visits, told me that my husband meant no real harm, that he was just confused and felt insecure. I was encouraged to be more tolerant and understanding. Most important, I was told to forgive him the beatings just as Christ had forgiven me from the cross. I did that, too.

Things continued. Next time I turned to a doctor. I was given little pills to relax me and told to take things a little easier. . . .

I turned to a friend, and when her husband found out, he accused me of either making things up or exaggerating the situation. She was told to stay away from me. She didn't, but she could no longer really help me. Just by believing me she was made to feel disloyal.

I turned to a professional family guidance agency. I was told there that my husband needed help and that I should find a way to control the incidents. I couldn't control the beatings—that was the whole point of my seeking help. At the agency I found I had to defend myself against the suspicion that I wanted to be hit, that I invited the beatings. Good God! Did the Jews invite themselves to be slaughtered in Germany?

I did go to two more doctors. One asked me what I had done to provoke my husband. The other asked if we had made up yet.

I called the police one time. They not only did not respond to the call, they called several hours later to ask if things had "settled down." I could have been dead by then!

I have nowhere to go if it happens again. No one wants to take in a woman with four children. Even if there were someone kind enough to care, no one wants to become involved in what is commonly referred to as a "domestic situation."

Everyone I have gone to for help has somehow wanted to blame me and vindicate my husband. I can see it lying there between their words and at the end of their sentences. The clergyman, the doctor, the counselor, my friend's husband, the police—all of them have found a way to vindicate my husband.

No one has to "provoke" a wife-beater. He will strike out when he's ready and for whatever reason he has at the moment.

I may be his excuse, but I have never been the reason.

I know that I do not want to be hit. I know, too, that I will be beaten again unless I can find a way out for myself and my children. I am terrified for them also.

. . . Staying with my husband means that my children must be subjected to the emotional battering caused when they see their mother's beaten face or hear her screams in the middle of the night.

I know that I have to get out. But when you have nowhere to go, you know that you must go on your own and expect no support. I have to be ready for that. I have to be ready to support myself and the children completely, and still provide a decent environment for them. I pray that I can do that before I am murdered in my own home. . . . I am still praying, and there is not a human person to listen.

29

DEIRDRE SILVERMAN

Sexual Harassment Begins with Hiring Procedures
1976

In the generations before the feminist movement, a woman's superiors at work could coerce sex in exchange for her keeping her job. As women moved into "nontraditional" jobs in the 1970s, some male coworkers also used unwelcome sexual advances to make them quit. The Civil Rights Act, by prohibiting employment discrimination, helped women to give a name — sexual harassment — to the problem. In 1980, with the black feminist and civil rights activist Eleanor Holmes Norton as its director, the Equal Employment Opportunity Commission announced that sexual harassment was henceforth illegal and offered employers guidelines on how to prevent it. The U.S. Supreme Court backed that judgment in 1985 when it ruled that such practices violated the civil rights of victims.

In May of 1975 Working Women United, an organization in Ithaca, New York, held a Speak-Out on Sexual Harassment. We defined sexual harassment as the treatment of women workers as sexual objects. This problem permeates all aspects of women's work.

Sexual harassment begins with hiring procedures, in which women applicants are judged not only for their work skills but also for their physical attractiveness (and, in some instances, sexual receptivity). It continues when job retention, raises or promotions depend on tolerating, or submitting to, unwanted sexual advances from co-workers, customers or supervisors. The form of these advances varies from clearly suggestive looks and/or remarks, to mild physical encounters (pinching, kissing, etc.) to outright sexual assault. In all instances, the message is clear: A woman's existence as a sexual being is more important than her work.

Respondents to a recent survey were asked to describe the most recent instance of sexual harassment they had experienced. The statistics

From *Quest* 3, no. 3 (Winter 1976–1977). Reprinted in Rosalyn Baxandall and Linda Gordon, eds., *Dear Sisters: Dispatches from the Women's Liberation Movement* (New York: Basic Books, 2000).

presented refer to the description each woman gave of that one instance. In more than half of the incidents described, the man or men doing the harassing were in work positions superior to the respondent. Another 18% were customers or clients. Thus, about two thirds of the men were in a position to exert some economic pressure on the respondent. In addition, 41% of the respondents described harassment involving more than one man.

In popular literature, sexual harassment is treated as a joke of little consequence. The actress who "succeeds" by means of the casting couch, the "Fly Me" airline stewardess and other stereotypes permeate American/male humor. Are women laughing along?

Respondents were asked to describe how they felt after being harassed. Table 1 shows their responses.

Many respondents indicated multiple reactions, so the percentage total is more than 100%. When asked, "Did this experience have any emotional or physical effect on you?", 78% answered yes. Consider the following comments:

"As I remember all the sexual abuse and negative work experiences I am left feeling sick and helpless and upset instead of angry."

"Reinforced feelings of no control—sense of doom."

"I have difficulty dropping the emotion barrier I work behind when I come home from work. My husband turns into just another man."

"Kept me in a constant state of emotional agitation and frustration. I drank a lot."

"Soured the essential delight in the work."

"Stomach ache, migraines, cried every night, no appetite."

Many women commented on how the harassment, or their reactions to it, interfered with their job performance. The economic consequences of impaired performance are difficult to measure. . . .

Ignoring the harassment is an ineffective response. For 76% of the respondents who tried this tactic the behavior continued, and sometimes got worse. In fact, almost one-third of these women were penalized on the job for not responding positively to the harassment. When asked why they didn't "complain through channels," women's responses indicated their weaknesses in the work situation. Forty-two percent felt that nothing would be done; 33% feared some negative consequences for themselves, varying from blame and ridicule to concrete penalties at work. For about 20% of the respondents, either there were no channels, or the harassing man was a part of them.

When respondents did officially complain, no action was taken in one third of the cases. One third of the respondents who complained

Table 1.   *Percent of Respondents Mentioning Each Reaction*

Angry	78%
Upset	48%
Frightened	23%
Guilty	22%
Flattered	10%
Indifferent	7%
Other (alienated, alone, helpless)	27%

were themselves penalized at work. In a small number of cases, action was taken against the man. The most severe of these was transfer to another work place or ejection of a customer.

When asked why they did not lodge formal complaints, respondents replied:

"I thought it was *my* problem."

"The importance I have been trained to place on what other people think of me—trying to please other people rather than finding my own rewards, fulfillment, etc."

"HoJo's pride themselves on their friendly, pretty girls—in a sense, they promote my sexual harassment." . . .

"No one would believe me."

"I felt I couldn't make a scene by telling anyone in authority over him. I felt powerless and, oddly, honor-bound not to publicly embarrass him."

"I would be seen as cruel and unprofessional."

When the sexual harassment issue surfaced in Ithaca last year, women's reactions were dramatically divided. Many expressed strong support along with relief that what had been seen as a personal problem was in fact a public issue. There was also, even from feminists, a certain amount of resistance. This was expressed in comments like:

"Any woman who has it together can handle something like that."

"That sort of thing only happens to women who are asking for it." (Often accompanied by, "It's never happened to me, because I know how to present myself.")

"Just because one weird guy does something that doesn't mean it's a real problem."

(These comments are all direct quotes from women I spoke with. Any resemblance to discussions of rape five years ago is not at all a coincidence.) . . .

At the Working Women United speak-out, women spoke about the "other side" of sexual harassment: being rejected as a worker because one is "unattractive." They felt resentment of the men in power who made those judgments, but they also felt resentment of the women who were hired because of the way they look. This jealousy and competition keeps women fighting among themselves, and not questioning the standards men are using or their right to use them.

Feminists should also regard sexual harassment as a workplace organizing issue. We should push for its recognition as a serious grievance, an intolerable working condition. We should make it clear that sexual exploitation of workers is not a joke.

Recognition and discussion of the issue in workplaces is important, so that women do not feel guilt or fear when they complain about sexual harassment. And it is important to provide organized support for individual cases, to follow up complaints and to insure the development of workplace policies that make sexual harassment unacceptable.

30

COMBAHEE RIVER COLLECTIVE

A Black Feminist Statement

1977

The most significant theoretical manifesto of black feminism came from the Combahee River Collective, an organization founded by Barbara Smith and others who considered the National Black Feminist Organization insufficiently radical. An example of socialist feminism, their statement articulated a politics based on the interlocking of the major systems of oppression—capitalism, patriarchy, racial hierarchy, and compulsory heterosexuality—that became the hallmark of black feminism. Expressing solidarity with black men as fellow victims of racism, the authors rejected the separatism of white lesbian feminists, even though some, like Smith, were lesbians. By 1977, when they produced this analysis, progressive activism of all kinds had begun to decline. Thus, the political

Reprinted in Zillah R. Eisenstein, ed., *Capitalist Patriarchy and the Case for Socialist Feminism* (New York: Monthly Review Press, 1979), 362–72.

sophistication expressed here was not easy to translate into mass action at the time, but it inspired fresh thinking that influenced later activism.

We are a collective of black feminists. . . . We are actively committed to struggling against racial, sexual, heterosexual, and class oppression and see as our particular task the development of integrated analysis and practice based upon the fact that the major systems of oppression are interlocking. The synthesis of these oppressions creates the conditions of our lives. As black women we see black feminism as the logical political movement to combat the manifold and simultaneous oppressions that all women of color face.

We will discuss four major topics in the paper that follows: (1) The genesis of contemporary black feminism; (2) what we believe . . . ; (3) the problems in organizing black feminists, including a brief herstory of our collective; and (4) black feminist issues and practice.

1. The Genesis of Contemporary Black Feminism

. . . We find our origins in the historical reality of Afro-American women's continuous life-and-death struggle for survival and liberation. Black women's extremely negative relationship to the American political system (a system of white male rule) has always been determined by our membership in two oppressed racial and sexual castes. . . . There have always been black women activists — some known, like Sojourner Truth, Harriet Tubman, Frances E. W. Harper, Ida B. Wells Barnett, and Mary Church Terrell, and thousands upon thousands unknown — who had a shared awareness of how their sexual identity combined with their racial identity to make their whole life situation and the focus of their political struggles unique. . . .

A black feminist presence has evolved most obviously in connection with the second wave of the American women's movement beginning in the late 1960s. Black, other Third World, and working women have been involved in the feminist movement from its start, but both outside reactionary forces and racism and elitism within the movement itself have served to obscure our participation. . . .

Black feminist politics also have an obvious connection to movements for black liberation, particularly those of the 1960s and 1970s. Many of us were active in those movements (civil rights, black nationalism, the Black Panthers), and all of our lives were greatly affected and changed by their ideology, their goals, and the tactics used to achieve their goals. It was our experience and disillusionment within these liberation movements, as well as experience on the periphery of the white male left, that led to the need to develop a politics that was antiracist, unlike those of white women, and antisexist, unlike those of black and white men.

There is also undeniably a personal genesis for black feminism. . . . Black feminists and many more black women who do not define themselves as feminists have all experienced sexual oppression as a constant factor in our day-to-day existence.

. . . In the process of consciousness-raising, actually life-sharing, we began to recognize the commonality of our experiences and, from that sharing and growing consciousness, to build a politics that will change our lives and inevitably end our oppression.

Our development also must be tied to the contemporary economic and political position of black people. The post–World War II generation of black youth was the first to be able to minimally partake of certain educational and employment options, previously closed completely to black people. Although our economic position is still at the very bottom of the American capitalist economy, a handful of us have been able to gain certain tools as a result of tokenism in education and employment which potentially enable us to more effectively fight our oppression.

A combined antiracist and antisexist position drew us together initially, and as we developed politically we addressed ourselves to heterosexism and economic oppression under capitalism.

2. What We Believe

Above all else, our politics initially sprang from the shared belief that black women are inherently valuable, that our liberation is a necessity not as an adjunct to somebody else's but because of our need as human persons for autonomy. . . . No other ostensibly progressive movement has ever considered our specific oppression a priority or worked seriously for the ending of that oppression. Merely naming the pejorative stereotypes attributed to black women (e.g., mammy, matriarch, Sapphire, whore, bulldagger), let alone cataloguing the cruel, often murderous, treatment we receive, indicates how little value has been placed upon our lives during four centuries of bondage in the Western hemisphere. We realize that the only people who care enough about us to work consistently for our liberation is us. . . .

This focusing upon our own oppression is embodied in the concept of identity politics. We believe that the most profound and potentially the most radical politics come directly out of our own identity as opposed to working to end somebody else's oppression. . . .

We believe that sexual politics under patriarchy is as pervasive in black women's lives as are the politics of class and race. We also often find it difficult to separate race from class from sex oppression because in our lives they are most often experienced simultaneously, . . . e.g., the history of rape of black women by white men as a weapon of political repression.

Although we are feminists and lesbians, we feel solidarity with progressive black men and do not advocate the fractionalization that white women who are separatists demand. Our situation as black people necessitates that we have solidarity around the fact of race. . . . We struggle together with black men against racism, while we also struggle with black men about sexism.

We realize that the liberation of all oppressed peoples necessitates the destruction of the political-economic systems of capitalism and imperialism as well as patriarchy. . . . We need to articulate the real class situation of persons who are not merely raceless, sexless workers, but for whom racial and sexual oppression are significant determinants in their working/economic lives. . . .

As we have already stated, we reject the stance of lesbian separatism because it is not a viable political analysis or strategy for us. It leaves out far too much and far too many people, particularly black men, women, and children. We have a great deal of criticism and loathing for what men have been socialized to be in this society: what they support, how they act, and how they oppress. But we do not have the misguided notion that it is their maleness, per se—i.e., their biological maleness— that makes them what they are. As black women we find any type of biological determinism a particularly dangerous and reactionary basis upon which to build a politic. We must also question whether lesbian separatism is an adequate and progressive political analysis and strategy . . . since it so completely denies any but the sexual sources of women's oppression, negating the facts of class and race.

3. Problems in Organizing Black Feminists

During our years together as a black feminist collective we have experienced success and defeat, joy and pain, victory and failure. We have found that it is very difficult to organize around black feminist issues, difficult even to announce in certain contexts that we *are* black feminists. . . . The major source of difficulty in our political work is that we are not just trying to fight oppression on one front or even two, but instead to address a whole range of oppressions. We do not have racial, sexual, heterosexual, or class privilege to rely upon, nor do we have even the minimal access to resources and power that groups who possess any one of these types of privilege have. . . .

If black women were free, it would mean that everyone else would have to be free since our freedom would necessitate the destruction of all the systems of oppression.

Feminism is, nevertheless, very threatening to the majority of black people because it calls into question some of the most basic assumptions about our existence, i.e., that gender should be a determinant of power relationships. . . .

The material conditions of most black women would hardly lead them to upset both economic and sexual arrangements that seem to represent some stability in their lives. Many black women have a good understanding of both sexism and racism, but because of the everyday constrictions of their lives cannot risk struggling against them both.

The reaction of black men to feminism has been notoriously negative. They are, of course, even more threatened than black women by the possibility that black feminists might organize around our own needs. They realize that they might not only lose valuable and hard-working allies in their struggles but that they might also be forced to change their habitually sexist ways of interacting with and oppressing black women. Accusations that black feminism divides the black struggle are powerful deterrents to the growth of an autonomous black women's movement.

Still, hundreds of women have been active at different times during the three-year existence of our group. And every black woman who came, came out of a strongly felt need for some level of possibility that did not previously exist in her life.

When we first started meeting early in 1974 after the NBFO first eastern regional conference, we did not have a strategy for organizing, or even a focus. . . .

Currently we are planning to gather together a collection of black feminist writing. We feel that it is absolutely essential to demonstrate the reality of our politics to other black women and believe that we can do this through writing and distributing our work. The fact that individual black feminists are living in isolation all over the country, that our own numbers are small, and that we have some skills in writing, printing, and publishing makes us want to carry out these kinds of projects as a means of organizing black feminists as we continue to do political work in coalition with other groups.

4. Black Feminist Issues and Practice

During our time together we have identified and worked on many issues of particular relevance to black women.... We might, for example, become involved in workplace organizing at a factory that employs Third World women or picket a hospital that is cutting back on already inadequate health care to a Third World community, or set up a rape crisis center in a black neighborhood. Organizing around welfare or daycare concerns might also be a focus....

Issues and projects that collective members have actually worked on are sterilization abuse, abortion rights, battered women, rape, and health care. We have also done many workshops and educationals on black feminism on college campuses, at women's conferences, and most recently for high school women.

One issue that is of major concern to us and that we have begun to publicly address is racism in the white women's movement. As black feminists we are made constantly and painfully aware of how little effort white women have made to understand and combat their racism, which requires among other things that they have a more than superficial comprehension of race, color, and black history and culture. Eliminating racism in the white women's movement is by definition work for white women to do, but we will continue to speak to and demand accountability on this issue.

... As feminists we do not want to mess over people in the name of politics. We believe in collective process and a nonhierarchical distribution of power within our own group and in our vision of a revolutionary society. We are committed to a continual examination of our politics as they develop through criticism and self-criticism as an essential aspect of our practice. As black feminists and lesbians we know that we have a very definite revolutionary task to perform and we are ready for the lifetime of work and struggle before us.

31

MEN ALLIED NATIONALLY FOR
THE EQUAL RIGHTS AMENDMENT

Ways Men Can Benefit from the ERA
1978

Many men supported the feminist movement. Polls found that both men and women, in roughly equal numbers, supported reforms such as ending sex discrimination in employment and ensuring the safety and legality of abortion. As conservative power grew, progressive male supporters became increasingly important in helping feminists fend off attacks, as this document illustrates.

1. Freedom from Being a Success Object

As men, we do not want to spend our lives supporting not only ourselves, but women, children (at $100,000 per child), a mortgage, and an image of ourselves.

Until women share that support we, as men, do not have the freedom to take risks on our job, or the freedom to fail taking those risks, for fear that if we do fail our family will end up in the poor house.

We cannot depend on women to share that support equally until women are paid equally. Nor can we expect women to share that support equally until women have equal access to trade union membership, to seniority positions within the unions, to in-house training for advancement once hired, to graduate education, law schools, medical schools and jobs at every level. And women cannot gain access to these jobs if the "buddy boy" system of hiring is not checked by affirmative action programs to balance the distorted hiring practices resulting from that system.

So, as the ERA helps check the distortion of hiring practices, men become freer to experiment with our lives—to escape the straight jacket of spending our lives getting the approval of the person above us at work so we can get to the next highest step on the ladder so we

---

Michael S. Kimmel and Thomas E. Mosmiller, eds., *Against the Tide: Pro-Feminist Men in the United States, 1776–1990* (Boston: Beacon Press, 1992), 422–24.

can get the next highest salary to support the next highest mortgage—a path that discourages men from asking ourselves "is this what I really want to be doing with my life?"

2. Child Nurturance

As the E.R.A. allows women the option to really share in the responsibilities of earning the income, it allows men more time to nurture our children.

3. Child Custody and Child Support

The E.R.A. will prevent states from depriving men of child custody merely because we are men. It will prevent us from being forced to declare our wives unfit mothers in order to gain equal access to custody. . . .

4. Alimony—Legality

The E.R.A. will make it illegal for states to automatically assign alimony payments to men based only on our sex. . . .

5. Alimony—Necessity

Courts will have less *reason* to assign alimony payments to men when women have had access to the training and income that makes alimony less necessary.

6. Divorce Training

When legal inequities push men into working outside the home and women into working inside the home this division of labor leads to a division of interests. The opposite interests push the sexes apart (e.g., the "opposite sex"), encouraging divorces. Training men and women to be opposite each other is, in essence, divorce training. . . .

7. Prostitutes and Security Objects

Women who hang onto relationships with men because society gives us the easier road to providing financial security make us into security objects and make themselves into prostitutes. . . .

8. Protective Labor Laws

The E.R.A. will allow extension to men of the protection of numerous labor laws in health, safety and overtime pay that now applies only to women. . . .

9. Inheritance

Many common law states require a husband to have a living child born of the marriage prior to receiving inheritance of his wife's realty. This is not required of the women. Women are hurt by other inheritance provisions. The ERA will force an equalization of these provisions.

10. Sexual Molestation of Boys

A number of states protect female children from adult male sexual molestation but do not protect male children from adult molestation by either sex. . . . The law should not eliminate boys from protection in clear cases of abuse while protecting females in such cases.

32

MITSUYE YAMADA

Asian Pacific American Women and Feminism

1979

The Immigration Act of 1965 ended the racially biased national origins quotas (established in 1924) and made immigration easier for Asians and others previously excluded. As their numbers grew, so did their political confidence. Japanese American and Chinese American women, who had the longest histories in the United States among Asian groups, led the way in articulating new feminist perspectives in the 1970s. Members of both groups had long suffered from racism in the United States and

Cherríe Moraga and Gloria Anzaldúa, *This Bridge Called My Back: Writings by Radical Women of Color* (Watertown, Mass.: Persephone Press, 1981), 71–75.

had been targets of hateful public policy. Both had important ties to developments in Asian politics. In this document, Mitsuye Yamada explains the concerns that led Asian American women to develop their own variants of feminism.

Most of the Asian Pacific American women I know agree that we need to make ourselves more visible by speaking out on the condition of our sex and race and on certain political issues which concern us. Some of us feel that visibility through the feminist perspective is the only logical step for us. However, this path is fraught with problems which we are unable to solve among us, because in order to do so, we need the help and cooperation of the white feminist leaders, the women who coordinate programs, direct women's buildings, and edit women's publications throughout the country. Women's organizations tell us they would like to have us "join" them and give them "input." These are the better ones; at least they know we exist and feel we might possibly have something to say of interest to them, but every time I read or speak to a group of people about the condition of my life as an Asian Pacific woman, it is as if I had never spoken before, as if I were speaking to a brand new audience of people who had never known an Asian Pacific woman who is other than the passive, sweet etc. stereotype of the "Oriental" woman.

. . . No matter what we say or do, the stereotype still hangs on. I am weary of starting from scratch each time I speak or write, as if there were no history behind us, of hearing that among the women of color, Asian women are the least political, or the least oppressed, or the most polite. It is too bad not many people remember that one of the two persons in Seattle who stood up to contest the constitutionality of the Evacuation Order in 1942 was a young Japanese American woman. As individuals and in groups, we Asian Pacific women have been (more intensively than ever in the past few years) active in community affairs and speaking and writing about our activities. . . . And yet, we continue to hear, "Asian women are of course traditionally not attuned to being political," as if most other women are; or that Asian women are too happily bound to their traditional roles as mothers and wives, as if the same cannot be said of a great number of white American women among us.

When I read . . . recently that at a workshop for Third World women in San Francisco, Cherríe Moraga exploded with "What each of us needs to do about what we don't know is to go look for it," I felt like standing up and cheering her. She was speaking at the Women's Building to a group of white sisters who were saying, in essence, "it is *your* responsibility as Third World women to teach *us*." If the majority culture knows so little about us, it must be *our* problem, they seem to be telling us; the burden of teaching is on us. I do not want to be unfair; I know individual women and some women's groups that have taken on the responsibility of teaching themselves through reaching out to women of color, but such gestures by the majority of women's groups are still tentatively made because of the sometimes touchy reaction of women who are always being asked to be "tokens" at readings and workshops.

Earlier this year, when a group of Asian Pacific American women gathered together in San Francisco poet Nellie Wong's home to talk about feminism, I was struck by our general agreement on the subject of feminism *as an ideal*. We all believed in equality for women. We agreed that it is important for each of us to know what it means to be a woman in our society, to know the historical and psychological forces that have shaped and are shaping our thoughts which in turn determine the directions of our lives. We agreed that feminism means a commitment to making changes in our own lives and a conviction that as women we have the equipment to do so. One by one, as we sat around the table and talked (we women of all ages ranging from our early twenties to the mid-fifties, single and married, mothers and lovers, straight women and lesbians), we knew what it was we wanted out of feminism, and what it was supposed to mean to us. For women to achieve equality in our society, we agreed, we must continue to work for a common goal.

But there was a feeling of disappointment in that living room toward the women's movement as it stands today. One young woman said she had made an effort to join some women's groups with high expectations but came away disillusioned because these groups were not receptive to the issues that were important to her as an Asian woman. . . . This pervasive feeling of mistrust toward the women in the movement is fairly representative of a large group of women who live in the psychological place we now call Asian Pacific America. A movement that fights sexism in the social structure must deal with racism, and we had hoped the leaders in the women's movement would be able to see the parallels in the lives of the women of color and themselves, and would "join" *us* in our struggle and give *us* "input."

It should not be difficult to see that Asian Pacific women need to affirm our own culture while working within it to change it. Many of the leaders in the women's organizations today had moved naturally from the civil rights politics of the 60's to sexual politics, while very few of the Asian Pacific women who were involved in radical politics during the same period have emerged as leaders in these same women's organizations. Instead they have become active in groups promoting ethnic identity, most notably ethnic studies in universities, ethnic theater groups or ethnic community agencies. This doesn't mean that we have placed our loyalties on the side of ethnicity over womanhood. The two are not at war with one another; we shouldn't have to sign a "loyalty oath" favoring one over the other. . . .

If I have more recently put my energies into the Pacific Asian American Center . . . and the Asian Pacific Women's Conferences (the first of its kind in our history), it is because the needs in these areas are so great. I have thought of myself as a feminist first, but my ethnicity cannot be separated from my feminism.

Through the women's movement, I have come to truly appreciate the meaning of my mother's life and the lives of immigrant women like her. My mother, at nineteen years of age, uprooted from her large extended family, was brought to this country to bear and raise four children alone. Once here, she found that her new husband who had been here as a student for several years prior to their marriage was a bachelor-at-heart and had no intention of changing his lifestyle. Stripped of the protection and support of her family, she found the responsibilities of raising us alone in a strange country almost intolerable during those early years. I thought for many years that my mother did not love us because she often spoke of suicide as an easy way out of her miseries. I know now that for her to have survived "just for the sake" of her children took great strength and determination.

If I digress it is because I, a second generation Asian American woman who grew up believing in the American Dream, have come to know who I am through understanding the nature of my mother's experience; . . . and through her I have become more sensitive to the needs of Third World women throughout the world. . . .

My politics as a woman are deeply rooted in my immigrant parent's and my own past. . . . As a child of immigrant parents, as a woman of color in a white society and as a woman in a patriarchal society, what is personal to me *is* political.

These are the connections we expected our white sisters to see. It should not be too difficult, we feel, for them to see why being a feminist activist is more dangerous for women of color. They should be able to see that political views held by women of color are often

misconstrued as being personal rather than ideological. Views critical
of the system held by a person in an "out group" are often seen as
expressions of personal angers against the dominant society. . . .

Remembering the blatant acts of selective racism in the past three
decades in our country, our white sisters should be able to see how
tenuous our position in this country is. Many of us are now third and
fourth generation Americans, but this makes no difference; periodic
conflicts involving Third World peoples can abruptly change white
Americans' attitudes towards us. . . .

Asian Pacific American women will not speak out to say what we
have on our minds until we feel secure within ourselves that this is
our home too; and until our white sisters indicate by their actions that
they want to join us in our struggle because it is theirs also. This
means a commitment to a truly communal education where we learn
from each other because we want to learn from each other, the kind of
commitment we do not seem to have at the present time. I am still
hopeful that the women of color in our country will be the link to
Third World women thoughout the world, and that we can help each
other broaden our visions.

33

JERRY FALWELL

Rise Up against the Tide of Permissiveness and Moral Decay

1980

*In the late 1970s and early 1980s, conservative white evangelical Chris-
tians entered politics as never before and soon became the most reliable
Republican voters. Like many Catholics, they opposed the ERA, legal
abortion, the ordination of women, and full citizenship for homosexuals.
Yet while the Catholic Church remained liberal on economic matters,
supported civil rights for racial minorities, and opposed the death*

From Jerry Falwell, *Listen, America!* (New York: Doubleday & Company, 1980), 7, 12,
13, 20–23, 121, 123–24, 128, 151, 180.

penalty and unjust wars, leading evangelical church leaders embraced big business and a militaristic foreign policy. Among the most famous was the Rev. Jerry Falwell, a Virginia Baptist, who founded the Moral Majority. Falwell and his fellow ministers tied advocacy of traditional gender roles and cultural conservatism to economic deregulation and an aggressive U.S. posture overseas, helping the Reagan administration change the terms of debate on domestic and foreign policies.

It is time that we come together and rise up against the tide of permissiveness and moral decay that is crushing in on our society from every side. America is at a crossroads as a nation; she is facing a fateful "Decade of Destiny"—the 1980s. I am speaking about survival and am calling upon those Americans who believe in decency . . . to face the truth that America is in trouble. . . .

Today government has become all-powerful as we have exchanged freedom for security. For all too many years, Americans have been educated to dependence rather than to liberty. A whole generation of Americans has grown up brainwashed by television and textbooks to believe that it is the responsibility of government to take resources from some and bestow them upon others. This idea certainly was alien to the Founding Fathers of our country. . . .

The free-enterprise system is clearly outlined in the Book of Proverbs in the Bible. Jesus Christ made it clear that the work ethic was a part of His plan for man. Ownership of property is biblical. Competition in business is biblical. Ambitious and successful business management is clearly outlined as a part of God's plan for His people. . . .

The hope of reversing the trends of decay in our republic now lies with the Christian public in America. We cannot expect help from the liberals. They certainly are not going to call our nation back to righteousness and neither are the pornographers, the smut peddlers, and those who are corrupting our youth. Moral Americans must be willing to put their reputations, their fortunes, and their very lives on the line for this great nation of ours. . . .

Americans must no longer linger in ignorance and apathy. We cannot be silent about the sins that are destroying this nation. The choice is ours. We must turn America around or prepare for inevitable destruction. . . .

The family is the God-ordained institution of the marriage of one man and one woman together for a lifetime with their biological or adopted children. The family is the fundamental building block and the basic unit of our society, and its continued health is a prerequisite for a healthy and prosperous nation. . . .

Too many men and women, trying to protect their own sinfulness and selfishness, are for the desires of self-gratification destroying the very foundation of the family as we know it.

In the war against the family today, we find an arsenal of weapons. The first weapon is the cult of the playboy, the attitude that has permeated our society in these last twenty years. This playboy philosophy tells men that they do not have to be committed to their wife and to their children, but that they should be some kind of a "cool, free swinger." . . . Men are satisfying their lustful desires at the expense of family.

The second weapon against the family is the feminist revolution. This is the counterreaction to the cult of the playboy. Many women are saying, "Why should I be taken advantage of by chauvinists? I will get out and do my own thing. I will stand up for my rights. I will have my own dirty magazines." Feminists are saying that self-satisfaction is more important than the family. Most of the women who are leaders in the feminist movement promote an immoral life style.

In a drastic departure from the home, more than half of the women in our country are currently employed. Our nation is in serious danger when motherhood is considered a task that is "unrewarding, unfulfilling, and boring." I believe that a woman's call to be a wife and mother is the highest calling in the world. . . .

The answer to stable families with children who grow up to be great leaders in our society and who themselves have stable homes will not come from . . . more part-time work for fathers and mothers, or parental leaves of absence, or thirty-hour weeks, or parental co-operatives and other forms of sharing childraising responsibilities. It will come only as men and women in America get in a right relationship to God and His principles for the home. . . .

Scripture declares that God has called the father to be the spiritual leader in his family. The husband is not to be the dictator of the family, but the spiritual leader. There is a great difference between a dictator and a leader. People follow dictators because they are forced to do so. They follow leaders because they want to. Good husbands who are godly men are good leaders. Their wives and children want to follow them and be under their protection. The husband is to be the decisionmaker and the one who motivates his family with love. . . .

I believe that at the foundation of the women's liberation movement there is a minority core of women who were once bored with life, whose real problems are spiritual problems. Many women have never accepted their God-given roles. They live in disobedience to God's laws and have promoted their godless philosophy throughout our society. God Almighty created men and women biologically different and with differing needs and roles. He made men and women to complement each other and to love each other. . . .

The Equal Rights Amendment is a delusion. . . . The Equal Rights Amendment can never do for women what needs to be done for them. Women need to know Jesus Christ as their Lord and Savior and be under His Lordship. They need a man who knows Jesus Christ as his Lord and Savior, and they need to be part of a home where their husband is a godly leader and where there is a Christian family. . . .

We as a nation must take a Bible position on morality and begin to teach it everywhere, beginning in our homes, in our schoolrooms, in our communities, and in our states.

34

CHARLOTTE BUNCH

Going beyond Boundaries

1985

As the Reagan presidency began to undermine hard-won reforms, some feminists expressed new appreciation of coalition. Progressives realized they could succeed only if they built alliances among varied groups in support of shared goals. Finding common ground, however, was not easy. One group might refuse to support a position that another group considered vital, and participants often found their encounters uncomfortable. But the conflicts taught the most committed activists important lessons about how to work across differences. Some began to apply that learning in working with feminists of other countries, as did Charlotte Bunch in this speech given in the lead-up to the United Nations Conference on Women in Nairobi, Kenya. Bunch had a long activist history that included civil rights and antiwar work, the radical University Christian

Karen Kahn, ed., *Frontline Feminism, 1975–1995: Essays from Sojourner's First 20 Years* (San Francisco: Aunt Lute Books, 1995), 453–58.

movement, and lesbian feminism. She became a leading voice for feminist progressive coalitions across borders, and in 1987 founded the Center for Women's Global Leadership at Rutgers University.

I have just returned from Peru, where I was involved in workshops that were a follow-up to the feminist *encuentro*, or meeting, held in Lima in 1983 with over 600 Latin American and Caribbean women present. At that time I was one of a handful of North Americans invited to offer ideas and developments from the women's movement in this country, but I hardly opened my mouth—I was overwhelmed by the things happening in Latin America. The energy reminded me, as a veteran of the early days of women's liberation in the United States, of the excitement and sense of discovery we felt then. I also realized something that is becoming more and more true: the latest burst of energy and ideas for feminism is coming from the Third World. (By that I mean both feminists in Third World countries and women of color in the United States, who are raising issues that are often similar to developments in Third World feminism.)

As a white U.S. feminist I celebrate this, because it brings insights and imagination that enable us to break some of the boundaries of our thinking—even though (as all of us who have been through various movement conflicts know) it isn't always easy to hear new ideas, or listen to criticisms of feminism in the last two decades. After three or four years of intense activity in one area, one of the best things you can do is listen to feminists emerging from some other place, whether it's Peru, New Zealand, a different part of the United States, or any other cultural context different from your own, even within the same city. Close attention to the perspectives and energy of women outside our own class, race, and culture helps us see more possibilities rather than fewer, to see what feminism can mean as we all grow and evolve a definition that goes beyond any particular cultural boundaries. Of course, no process of taking diversity seriously and listening to different points of view is without challenge, discomfort, and conflict, but I think it's well worth the price.

Understanding this process will be especially crucial at the U.N. conferences in Kenya in July, although I think it will be much more possible to do at the nongovernmental meeting than at the governmental one. The U.N. graciously declared 1975 "International Women's Year," and sponsored an international women's conference in Mexico City that was in many ways the first acknowledgment of women as a global force. A "Decade for Women" was announced after the recognition in Mexico

City that the elimination of women's oppression would take more than a year, and a "mid-decade" conference was held in 1980 in Copenhagen. Now we're at the end of the decade, and progress for women seems in many ways to have been minimal; poverty is increasing among women worldwide, there has been very little significant rise in the political power of women—and these are only two of the hard statistical problems we face at this "end of the decade."

But there has been enormous growth in the women's movement during the last ten years: we see women everywhere defining their reality for themselves. To me, the first step in taking any kind of power in any culture is refusing to accept the patriarchal definition of who you are and what your reality is, and this is the stage that I think most women in the world—including this country—are in. But as we each define our own reality, we also must recognize women's diversity. The first step, "We are women, we are distinct, we are oppressed, and there is a women's consciousness"—then must lead almost instantly to, "And yet at the same time there is no one 'women's reality,' except perhaps in the general fact of the subordination of women in every culture—a subordination that takes many varying cultural and individual forms." So the stage of seeing ourselves as similar, seeing ourselves as women, and feeling the excitement of being in a group is followed by the more difficult realization that as a group we are a multitude of groups who are not always united. The struggle for unity requires first recognizing and examining our differences and then asking which of those are strengths and which are simply based on oppression.

It seems clear to me, however, that at the Kenya conferences the worldwide media will use these very differences to say that women are hopelessly divided and that feminism is dead. Our diversity—a source of potential strength—will be manipulated by forces that do not wish to see feminism thrive. But I'm hoping that, in the midst of all the predictable conflicts in Kenya, a number of women will do what we've done over and over in the past decade: build networks around shared concerns, places where we can see our common oppression and work together to solve it. Recently I've worked mostly in the area of sexual violence against women, but coalition building has also happened in many other areas, such as in the women's health movement and among women working in rural development, including U.S. women who face conditions similar to those in some so-called "developing" countries.

By the way, I hope one of the first items on our agenda will be elimination of language like "developed" and "developing": the condescending notion that the Western industrialized world is "developed" is highly questionable outside any but a strictly industrialized interpretation of that word. For lack of a better phrase, I refer to most of the nations of Asia, Latin America, and Africa called "developing countries" as the "Third World," an equally difficult term, but one that at least suggests the possibility of nonalignment with the U.S./U.S.S.R. blocs. This question of terminology raises the related issue of how women, as we define ourselves, can also redefine the ways in which the world is categorized. At the United Nations—created initially to be a place of world unity—you see especially clearly how the various power blocs have developed and solidified. It is very difficult for women there to talk across governmental and bloc lines. The official U.N. conference is a meeting of over 150 patriarchies, not a gathering of the women of those countries or women who see themselves beyond nation state definitions. The official Kenya conference will be women and men representing patriarchal governments without the freedom to speak what they feel and think—and this is as true of the U.S. delegation as any other. As we saw in Copenhagen, delegates will be pulled in whenever they start to talk beyond bloc lines. Under these circumstances, we cannot expect much more than a reading on how governments view women from the official U.N. conference in Nairobi.

But the NGO Forum can be quite a different matter. I see women there being able to break down barriers, because we will not be under the same obligations to state powers and can examine our positions and the divisions between us. In fact, this conference may be unique because of the emergence of feminism in the Third World in recent years. In 1980, feminism was a term that most women in Third World countries were afraid of, or didn't like, or rejected completely because the media had portrayed feminists with the kinds of stereotypes we know so well in this country. We were described as women who only wanted to get to the top within an oppressive world power system— and why would peasants in Latin America identify with a few women trying to become the head of General Motors? We were also caricatured as crazies, women who hated men, lesbians who couldn't have men, and so on. Feminism has been ridiculed and stereotyped worldwide, and the issues we have raised have usually not been taken seriously by the media.

But remarkably, despite this bad press, feminism has continued to grow. Women's groups all over the world, but especially in the Third World, are taking up issues ranging from housing, nutrition, and poverty to militarism, sexual and reproductive freedom, and violence against women. We face these issues in the United States, too, of course, but their forms vary depending on the culture and where women feel the most intense oppression at any moment. For example, women in shantytowns around Lima, who live on the very edge of survival, are organizing communal kitchens called *comedores populares*, or "popular restaurants." In their traditional role as food providers, they are creating a means to feed their families that is leading them to challenge the whole structure of society and the basis for survival. In shopping together to get better prices, they are starting to ask questions about inflation—why, when food is grown so close to their homes, is it so expensive—and about the worldwide food business in which many countries export certain foods as cash crops while their people starve. And in fixing meals together, they are evolving a sense of community, of being together as women; one group, after talking about violence in the neighborhood, set up a system in which a woman blows a whistle if she is being beaten.

This is only one example of the many ways in which women around the world are saying, "We will no longer be silent about any part of our lives in which we are oppressed." And that statement makes very clear that there is no such thing as a separate "women's issue," although there are women's special concerns and women's perspectives. When we talked about "women's issues" early in the women's movement, we were trying to place on the political agenda things women cared about that had not been considered political: equal rights, reproductive freedom, lesbian rights, child care, violence against women. But we have to say today that all of these are issues of human justice, of human society, not just women's issues.

And, as important, all of the concerns which have been called "larger issues" must be considered women's issues. This became especially clear to me at the Copenhagen conference, where a Western woman said that to talk feminism to a woman who has no home, no food, and no water is to talk nonsense. A group of us, feminists from both Western and Third World countries, wrote a response pointing out that feminism has to do with everything in the world, and so *is* a perspective on food, home, and water. But we also saw the challenge in what she said: if her words become true, then feminism will not fulfill its potential to be a transforming force in the world, although it may do some useful things. I'm hopeful that in Kenya this summer a larger body of women than ever before will develop feminist perspectives on issues like food, shelter, and water.

I also hope that U.S. feminists there will avoid some of the traps that we often fall into, like the tendency to relate to global feminism from one of two extremes. One is to be guilty and overapologetic, to say, in effect, "I have nothing to say because my country is so terrible that nothing I could offer would ever be of use to anybody anywhere

else. Please tell me what I should do, and I'll do anything you tell me."
Nobody wants that; it's not a partnership, not a real sharing and learning, not the kind of connection that feminism is all about. It may be
useful to somebody to have your help, but that approach is patronizing
and not the basis of fundamental change. The opposite attitude is
"feminist imperialism," which implies, "Feminism started in the United
States, after all. We will show you the way. You're in a stage in a process that we've already gone through, and five years from now you'll
agree that we were right." I hope we'll be able to say instead, "My experience is valuable and authentic, and I will share it. But I also want
to learn about what others are doing, and, without feeling guilty, I
want to see where I have been culture-bound and how I can go
beyond my particular boundaries." The point isn't to browbeat ourselves or to get defensive if, for example, somebody points out something as racist; the point is to try to understand what that means and
begin working to change it. Such a stance—which is not so unnatural,
and can actually be quite loving—will be crucial in Kenya.

We will also need to bring home from there what we learn from this
approach. We don't want to be "international experts" who no longer
relate to our own country, a nation which is, after all, one of the
problems in the world. We have to address what the United States
does, rather than simply feel apologetic or defensive about it—and we
have to look at how our work as feminists affects people's lives worldwide. For example, when U.S. women succeeded ten years ago in getting certain birth control devices outlawed, we didn't understand,
because we didn't have a global consciousness, that they would simply
be dumped on women in the Third World; I think we know now that if
we're going to ban things from the shores of the United States, we
also have to make sure they're destroyed. And we will increasingly be
concerned about people in other countries not just because "we ought
to be," but because we're all so closely connected: secretaries who
form a union may lose their jobs when their company responds by
sending clerical work via satellite to Barbados, where it can pay starvation wages—thus exploiting two groups of women.

There is a group of women on the Mexico-Texas border working
against the manipulation of women's jobs back and forth across that
border, and this is the kind of networking we will have to do if feminism is to continue to grow and to realize its global potential. [That]
dialogue must happen in the '80s and '90s if feminism is to reach
toward those solutions and respond to the world's enormous need for
new perspectives based on women's experiences.

35

YOICHI SHIMATSU AND PATRICIA LEE

Dust and Dishes: Organizing Workers
1989

In 1989, women—usually African American, Latina, or Asian immigrants—and their children comprised the major part of the working poor. Most of those who worked full time but still struggled to make ends meet were employed in the rapidly expanding service and retail sectors. Some looked to unions for aid in improving their lives, often making antidiscrimination clauses a key part of their contract demands, as this story of Asian American women in San Francisco's luxury hotel district illustrates.

On Nob Hill the Christmas holidays are a fancy affair. Limousines glide past antique cable cars to deliver partygoers to grand hotels. Inside, the pastry chefs have constructed a life-sized gingerbread house for the children. . . .

Behind the scenes, however, Asians and other immigrants carry on the more mundane work of operating a major hotel. Every morning at sunrise, Asian workers trudge up the steep grade from neighboring Chinatown or nearby bus stops to clock in at employee entrances. Inside cavernous kitchens, cooks fire up ovens and start the coffee while buspersons prepare table settings of china, flowers, and real silverware. Room cleaners push their carts by linen stations to pick up fresh sheets and towels. Before any of the guests wake up, another workday has begun. . . .

Unsuk Perry, a Korean American room cleaner, recalled her first day on the job at a downtown hotel. "I had never been employed before, so I was ready for anything. I didn't expect the work to be so hard physically, especially turning over the mattresses. It took a long time to get used to such work. The other employees were friendly and

---

Asian Women United of California, eds., *Making Waves: An Anthology of Writings by and about Asian American Women* (Boston: Beacon Press, 1989), 386–95.

helped me along. Most of them were immigrants, too, so they understood how I felt."

. . . As a union shop steward, she frequently translates for her
Korean co-workers. "During lunch breaks, I explain to them our
union's medical and dental plan for their families. It takes about five
years for the newer non-English-speaking women to fully adjust to
their jobs and fit in with the rest of the employees," she noted. Perry's
ability to help her colleagues stems not only from her years of experience, but also from leadership training and counseling that she received from a community-based group which helps Asian immigrant
women working in entry-level jobs.

. . . Within the hotel business, . . . job categories are basically
divided into two tracks: the "back of the house" or less visible, lower
paying positions, such as room cleaner, buspersons, and dishwashers;
and the "front of the house" or high visibility, tipped jobs and skilled
crafts, including bartenders, food and cocktail servers, and chefs. The
wage gap between the two tracks can be extremely wide, with chefs
earning double the pay of room cleaners. There exists a corresponding
hierarchy in social status where white Americans and Europeans are
clustered in the higher ranking positions.

The inequity in wages and social status was the main cause of the
organizing movement among San Francisco Asian and Latina room
cleaners in the late 1970s. Although physically isolated from each
other on the job, the room cleaners maintained a high level of cama-
raderie at impromptu meetings in the employees' cafeteria and
women's locker room. . . .

During the two-year period of arbitration and contract negotiation
from 1978 to 1980, the Asian and Latina room cleaners won a series
of victories, including an unprecedented 44 percent wage increase, a
reduction of workload by one room per day, free meals, a grievance
procedure, and a shop steward system. One main problem remained:
what the women workers felt to be the management's overbearing
attitude towards them. The local press described the 1980 hotel strike
which followed as a fight for "dignity and respect." After the month-
long strike, the room cleaners returned to work with an improved
sense of worth and self-esteem, and with hopes that they would never
again be discounted by either the management or the union.

Other Asian women in the hotels have also developed affirmative
action strategies to challenge sex and race barriers. Behind a gleam-
ing stainless steel counter, Filipina American cook Lina Abellan

decorates trays of small cakes with floral designs of whipped cream and chocolate frosting. As a *garde manger*, or garnish chef, she applies her artistry to fancy relishes, ice carvings, and other ornamental arrangements.

She is also fighting for fair promotions at her downtown hotel. "Hotel management has this mistaken idea that it's classier to have European or white American chefs. Whenever there's an opening for a sous chef's position, managers will usually pass up a qualified minority applicant even if they have to hire from the outside," she explained. "Other minority cooks and I have applied unsuccessfully for a chef's position, myself five times. Frankly, we are getting tired of training inexperienced outsiders who were supposed to supervise us."

A black shop steward advised her to file a complaint with the state Fair Employment and Housing Commission. After reviewing her case, the commission authorized her to initiate a civil lawsuit under Title VII of the Civil Rights Act, which prohibits employment discrimination. With the assistance of an Asian American community legal group, Abellan and her co-workers are preparing a class action suit. "Filipino and other minority cooks don't really want to 'rock the boat,' but sometimes you don't have any other choice. Whatever it takes—in the union or in court—we must make sure that everyone is treated fairly and equally," she said.

Abellan has demonstrated the same level of commitment and leadership within her union. In early 1985 she successfully ran for the executive board with a multi-ethnic reform slate. . . .

One of just a handful of Asian American women union leaders, Abellan admits she still has much to learn. "Parliamentary procedure, financial matters, policy issues . . . these are all very new to me. It's a big responsibility to represent such a large membership. Now I can appreciate the importance of support from the rank and file." Since Local 2 of the Hotel and Restaurant Workers Union is the city's largest labor organization, with thirteen thousand members, her leadership role has a direct influence on the future of many San Francisco–area working women.

36

JYOTSNA VAID

Seeking a Voice: South Asian Women's Groups in North America

1989

As the number of South Asian women grew in the United States and Canada by the late 1970s, some formed organizations to bring their concerns to the attention of their communities and the wider women's movement. This survey shows the great variety among the groups, as well as the common issues and challenges.

Although numerous regional associations of immigrants from South Asia exist all across North America, ... there has been a noticeable lack of attention to the particular concerns of women immigrants from the Indian subcontinent. ...

However, over the past decade a number of women, recognizing the need for a separate forum for articulating their unique concerns, have formed autonomous grassroots organizations in different parts of the United States and Canada. More than a dozen of these groups have sprung up. Founded by and composed entirely of women, these groups highlight the experiences, concerns, and contributions of women from the Indian subcontinent. ...

Who are these groups? How did they form? What areas have their members determined to most need services? And what internal problems have they encountered at various stages of development? ...

The eleven groups surveyed for this essay are located across the continent, three in Canada and eight in the United States. The oldest group was founded in 1980, the newest in 1985. The groups are relatively small, ranging in size from just two or three to fifteen core members. All of the members are middle-class women in their mid-twenties to early-fifties. ... The women tend to be highly educated, most either

Asian Women United of California, *Making Waves: An Anthology of Writings by and about Asian American Women* (Boston: Beacon Press, 1989), 395–405.

possessing or pursuing graduate degrees. . . . The group's core members include few women who work at home or in working-class occupations. Most of the group members emigrated from India, although a few of them are from Pakistan, Nepal, Sri Lanka, and Bangladesh. . . .

Although all the groups surveyed are concerned with promoting the status of women, their orientation and priorities—which reflect the factors leading to their formation—differ. For one set of groups, events in the Indian subcontinent, such as dowry-related deaths or the impact of Islamization on women's legal rights, served as the impetus. These groups formed to work with women's groups located in South Asia. A second category includes groups which were mobilized by a desire to address specific problems experienced by South Asian women immigrants, such as domestic violence, unequal social and economic opportunities, or discrimination. The last set of organizations formed because the members wished to establish a visible identity, whether along lines of ethnicity or sexual preference. . . .

The survey . . . asked whether the groups perceived themselves as "feminist" groups. Responses to the question were evenly divided. Anamika members stated that although they consider themselves feminists, the women they hope to reach may or may not be so. The woman in Los Angeles who responded on behalf of the Asian Indian Women's Network explained that she would not refer to her group as feminist because the "women are still not ready." . . .

The services and activities offered reflect what these women feel are the priorities for their community. . . . The activities fall into four general categories: (1) information, referral, and networking; (2) counseling and crisis intervention; (3) direct social services; and (4) advocacy on issues affecting women's rights.

Activities may focus on issues in South Asia or North America. For instance the Committee on South Asian Women has donated books and given small grants to autonomous women's groups in South Asia and sponsored visits by feminists from these groups. . . . Many of the groups have used newsletters and other publications to disseminate information about South Asian women from their own perspective. . . .

Despite the groups' achievements, members acknowledge that they have met with some problems, ranging from the pragmatic to the ideological. One of the most obvious and most prevalent problems is financial insecurity. . . . Another obstacle is limited time. . . .

The respondent from the Asian Indian Women's Network in Los Angeles cited "lack of support from spouses" as one of the most controversial internal problems of her group. . . .

Last but not least is the difference of opinion about the philosophy of the women's group, a difference that can be characterized as a "struggle versus service" debate. . . . For those who embrace a feminist perspective, . . . it becomes a serious problem if their efforts are directed toward providing short-term relief, which only helps their clients adapt to the status quo that keeps them subjugated.

Most groups have not yet resolved all these issues, but increasingly recognize the necessity of periodic self-appraisal. They also agree that to achieve their goals sister organizations need to improve mutual coordination and cooperation.

37

LAURIE OUELLETTE

Building the Third Wave: Reflections of a Young Feminist
1992

The generation of women who were born in the 1970s came of age in the 1990s. Some young feminists called themselves the "third wave" to distinguish from the "second-wave" of their mothers' generation and the "first-wave" suffragists. As college students and recent graduates, they tended to place issues of sexuality and cultural representation high on their agendas, while also sharing other feminists' social justice concerns. The author of this document, then a student and now a professor of communications studies, describes her personal experience, while, ironically, treating some media stereotypes of 1970s feminism as fact.

I am a member of the first generation of women to benefit from the gains of the 1970s' women's movement without having participated in its struggles. I grew up on the sidelines of feminism—too young to

On the Issues 24 (Fall 1992): 9–11, 60.

take part in those moments, debates and events that would define the women's movement, while at the same time experiencing firsthand the societal changes that feminism had demanded.

. . . I never really thought much about feminism as I was growing up but, looking back, I believe I've always had feminist inclinations. Having divorced parents, and a father who was ambivalent about his parental responsibilities, probably has much to do with this. I was only five when my parents separated in 1971, and I couldn't possibly have imagined or understood the E.R.A. marches, consciousness-raising groups, or triumphal passing of *Roe v. Wade* that shortly would make history. Certainly I couldn't have defined the word *feminism*. Still, watching my young mother struggle emotionally and financially as a single parent made the concept of gender injustice painfully clear, teaching me a lesson which would follow me always.

My first real introduction to feminism came secondhand. During the height of the '70s' women's movement, I watched my mother become "liberated" after the breakup of yet another marriage. It was she, not I, who sought some answers from the counterculture of the time. It was confusing, if not terrifying, to watch her change her life dramatically—and, by association, mine—during those years, transforming herself into a woman I barely recognized. She quit her job and returned to college and then graduate school, working odd jobs and devoting her time to books and meetings and new-age therapy and talking it all out with her never-ending supply of free-spirited divorced comrades. I was 13 the year I found her copy of *The Women's Room*, a book which so intrigued me that I read it cover to cover in the course of only a few nights. Like the heroine of the book, my mother was becoming "independent" and "hip," but I had never been so miserable.

Like most women my age, though, I never really considered feminism in terms of my own life until I reached college. It was during those years that I first took an interest in feminist classics like *The Feminine Mystique, Sisterhood is Powerful* and *Sexual Politics*. As powerful as these texts were, they seemed to express the anger of an earlier generation, simultaneously captivating and excluding me. Reading them so long after the excitement of their publication made my own consciousness-raising seem anticlimatic. These books, and countless others that I encountered, seemed to speak more to my mother's generation than mine. . . . I, like many of my white, middle-class friends, saw women's liberation from quite a different perspective. Many of us

really believed that we wouldn't have to worry about issues like discrimination, oppression, and getting stuck in the housewife role....

Although I participated in feminist activities sporadically in college,
including prochoice demonstrations, it was . . . outside that environment where my feminist politics took root. Several events stand out as
catalysts. First was an internship I held at a public television station
while in college. Armed with an eager attitude and practical experience, I felt my enthusiasm wane when I was given mainly menial and
secretarial tasks to perform while my male co-interns, who had less
experience than I, were frequently asked to do editing assignments
and were invited along on shoots. I had never before experienced sexual discrimination, and, in fact, honestly believed it was something I
would never have to face. In retrospect, this experience marked my
first realization that there was much work to be done in creating a
world where women and men were treated with equal respect, on the
job and off.

Living in an inner-city neighborhood, and my involvement in community issues there, was also important. I saw the dire need for drastic
political change in the lives of the poor women, elderly women, and
women of color who were my neighbors. Watching these women,
many of them single parents, struggling daily to find shelter, childcare,
and food made me realize that they, unlike me, had not been touched
at all by the gains of the '70s' women's movement. How could women's
liberation possibly be perceived as won when these women had been
so forgotten? I began to reconsider feminism in an attempt to find the
answers.

Today I am among the minority of young women who have committed
themselves to feminism in the hopes of achieving social and political
goals for all women. While we are attempting to carve out a place for
ourselves in a movement still heavily dominated by another generation,
the majority of young women have been reluctant to do the same. Confused about their roles in relation to the media stereotypes about feminists or intimidated by the legacy of the women's movement past, many
have become "no, but" feminists. That is, they approve of—indeed,
demand—equal pay, economic independence, sexual freedom and
reproductive choice, but are still reluctant to define themselves with the
label "feminist." The results of a recent poll by *In View*, a magazine for
college women, is typical of many surveys that report this contradiction.
According to the 514 female undergraduates surveyed by *In View*,
90 percent agreed that men and women should earn equal pay for equal

work; 93 percent said that women want equality with men; 84 percent agreed that women should have access to birth control, regardless of age or marital status; 90 percent believed that sexism still exists. Still, only 16 percent of the women said they were definitely feminists.

Yet the evidence clearly shows that young women's situations are dismal. *Roe v. Wade* is under fire, and if overturned will impact most on my generation and those to come; parental consent laws, which require parental notification or permission for abortion, have been mandated in many states, date rape and violence against women have become epidemics on college campuses and everywhere; eating disorders, linked to the unreasonable societal standards for women's body sizes, have claimed the lives of thousands of us; and we still can expect to earn 70 cents on every dollar earned by men. Sure, our chances of having professional careers are greater. However, more of us than in any previous generation have grown up in single-parent families—we have seen the myth of the "supermom" professional "bringing home the bacon and frying it up in a pan" and can call it for what it is. In these hard economic times, young women can look forward to mandatory full-time jobs and second shifts of housecare and childcare in their homes. Where are the parental-leave policies, the flexible schedules, the adequate healthcare, the subsidized day-cares, and the male cooperation that will ease these situations? . . .

Given all this, what can explain why so many young women have shunned feminism? In her survey of young women, *Feminist Fatale: Voices from the Twentysomething Generation Explore the Future of the Women's Movement*, Paula Kamen found that media-fueled stereotypes of feminists as "man-bashers" and "radical extremists" were behind the fact that many young women don't identify with the women's movement.

But these are not the only reasons. Kamen also points to the lack of young feminist role models as an important factor. The failure of major feminist organizations such as N.O.W. to reach out to a wider spectrum of women, including young women, must be acknowledged as a part of this problem. While individual chapters do have young feminist committees and, sometimes, officers, they and the national office are led and staffed primarily by older women, and consequently often fail to reflect the interests and needs of a complex generation of young women.

Yet another reason young women have turned away from feminism may lie within its history. If the young women who have gained the most from feminism—that is, white, middle-class women who took advantage of increased accessibility to higher education and professional employment—have been reluctant to associate themselves with feminism, it is hardly surprising that most economically disadvantaged women and women of color, who have seen fewer of those gains, have not been eager to embrace feminism either. . . .

Only by making issues of class and race a priority can feminism hope to impact on the lives of the millions of women for whom the daily struggle to survive, not feminist activism, is a priority. Will ours be the first generation of feminists to prioritize fighting cuts in Aid to Families with Dependent Children, establishing the right to national healthcare, daycare, and parental leave, and bringing to the forefront other issues pertinent to the daily struggle of many women's lives? If there is to be a third wave of feminism, we must.

While the women's movement of the '70s focused primarily on the E.R.A., getting women into high-paying, powerful occupations and combatting sexual discrimination in the workplace, these issues—while still critical—must not be the only goals of feminism. My sister is an example. . . . She has chosen . . . for now . . . marrying young and raising a family. Does she signify a regression into the homemaker role of the 1950s? On the contrary. In fact, she is among those feminists that I most respect, even though she herself believes that the feminist movement may not have a place for her because of the choices she has made. For her, issues such as getting midwifery legalized and covered by insurance plans, providing information about the importance of breastfeeding to rural mothers, countering the male-dominated medical establishment by using and recommending natural and alternative healing methods, protecting the environment and raising her own daughter with positive gender esteem are central to what she defines as a feminist agenda. Who am I to say that she—and other young women like her who are attempting to reclaim the power and importance of motherhood—aren't correct? If there is to be a third wave of feminism, it must acknowledge and support a wide range of choices for all women.

Surely the greatest challenge facing all young women is the frightening assault on reproductive rights, and if any issue can unite women from all backgrounds it is this. While we have never known the horrors of coat-hanger abortions, we have seen our reproductive rights drastically shrink. If the legacy of the women's movement has left young women confused about their roles in a structure still heavily dominated by older white women, this is one issue on which the torch

must be shared. If feminism is to succeed in challenging this patriarchal assault on women's bodies, a coalition of women from all backgrounds will have to join forces to address the underlying assumptions
of this attack. Young women have been among the first to organize on
this fight, witnessed by the proliferation of prochoice activity on college campuses. Still, if this movement is to progress beyond a single-
issue campaign, uniting women inside and outside the academy in the
name of feminism, it will mean expanding the agenda: Insisting upon
birth control options for all women, and giving equal energy to
addressing the lack of educational opportunities, childcare, daycare,
and healthcare options fundamental to the campaign for reproductive
choice.

Only by recognizing and helping provide choices for all women,
and supporting all women in their struggles to obtain those choices,
will the women of my generation, the first raised in the shadow of the
second wave and witness [to] its triumphs and failures, be able to
build a successful third wave of the feminist movement. The initial
step must be to reclaim the word *feminism* as an appealing, empower-
ing term in women's lives by building a movement that commits to all
women, while recognizing their multiple concerns.

38

CANDACE STEELE

PFLAG Supports Gay and Lesbian Children
1994

Over the past two decades, solidarity with lesbians and gays confront-
ing harassment has emerged as a new form of activism. High school stu-
dents in particular have been active in gay-straight alliances to combat
the often vicious homophobia of fellow students and the repression of
discussion about sexual orientation by school administrators. On college

Voters' Pamphlet, State of Oregon General Election November 8, 1994, 77, 78, 85, 90.
Reprinted in *Gay and Lesbian Rights in the United States: A Documentary History,* ed.
Walter L. Williams and Yolanda Retter (Westport, Conn.: Greenwood Press, 2003),
226–27.

*campuses, too, students have found the forums created by such groups
congenial for developing a larger gender critique. Parents, sometimes
prompted by antigay violence against their own children, have organized
to change bigoted attitudes and policies. In this selection, Candace
Steele, of Parents, Families and Friends of Lesbians and Gays (PFLAG),
spoke out against an antigay ballot initiative by Oregon conservatives.
Called Measure 13, it aimed to deny civil rights protections to lesbians
and gay men and to censor school curricula on sexuality.*

My family is one of hundreds in Oregon which have beloved children and
other cherished family members who happen to be gay or lesbian. In
the shadows are thousands of other Oregonians who fear discrimination for themselves and their loved ones in the climate of intolerance
and prejudice that this measure creates.

Our loved ones right now can be fired from the jobs they compe-
tently perform, or can be forced from their homes, simply because
they are gay or are perceived to be gay. Today in Oregon this is
perfectly legal. This ballot measure's intent and action is to make
permanent this discrimination against our families. It specifically targets homosexuals as the only group to be barred forever from protection against intolerance and prejudice. This measure violates our
nation's constitutional principles of equal protection.

Our loved ones do not ask for quotas nor affirmative action. These
are specifically prohibited in the Oregon State Constitution. What they
seek are exactly the same protections that all other citizens of Oregon
and the United States possess. In the name of basic justice, prevent
this senseless wrong! Vote no on 13!

Our gay and lesbian young people do not choose their orientation,
nor are they recruited by others. Our gay teens are often taunted,
physically attacked, and sometimes killed. They are told lies that they
are worthless and evil. They survive in isolation and fear, dropping out
of school, and running away from home. Some are driven to alcohol
and drugs, or to suicide. This cruel, mean-spirited measure permanently denies them accurate knowledge about themselves. Other children will grow up in the ignorance that leads to bigotry. Will you
destroy the hope of all our children to be productive and valued? *All*
children, ours and yours, need and deserve love and respect. Please
vote no on 13 to nurture all Oregon's children.

39

BEIJING DECLARATION AND PLATFORM FOR ACTION

Women's Rights Are Human Rights

1995

By century's end, feminism had spread and deepened throughout the world, thanks to communication across national borders among activists who learned from one another's experiences and ideas. With the increase in nongovernmental organizations (NGOs) that addressed human rights and economic development issues in this period, feminism became an important part of the process. In 1995, the largest international feminist assembly in world history gathered in Beijing, China, under United Nations auspices. The conference, which attracted 7,000 attendees from the United States, formal delegations from 189 countries, and over 2,000 NGOs, produced a wide-ranging Declaration and Platform of Action, excerpted here. Animated by the recognition that women's rights were an indivisible and essential part of human rights, it warned that increasing poverty and warfare threatened both.

1. We, the Governments participating in the Fourth World Conference on Women,
2. Gathered here in Beijing in September 1995, the year of the fiftieth anniversary of the founding of the United Nations,
3. Determined to advance the goals of equality, development and peace for all women everywhere in the interest of all humanity,
4. Acknowledging the voices of all women everywhere and taking note of the diversity of women and their roles and circumstances, honoring the women who paved the way and inspired by the hope present in the world's youth,
5. Recognize that the status of women has advanced in some important respects in the past decade but that progress has been uneven, inequalities between women and men have

From United Nations, "Beijing Declaration and Platform for Action," from the Fourth United Nations Conference on Women (New York: UN, 2001).

persisted and major obstacles remain, with serious consequences for the well-being of all people,

6. Also recognize that this situation is exacerbated by the increasing poverty that is affecting the lives of the majority of the world's people, in particular women and children, with origins in both the national and international domains,

7. Dedicate ourselves unreservedly to addressing these constraints and obstacles and thus enhancing further the advancement and empowerment of women all over the world, and agree that this requires urgent action in the spirit of determination, hope, cooperation and solidarity, now and to carry us forward into the next century. . . .

WE ARE CONVINCED THAT:

13. Women's empowerment and their full participation on the basis of equality in all spheres of society, including participation in the decision-making process and access to power, are fundamental for the achievement of equality, development and peace;

14. Women's rights are human rights;

15. Equal rights, opportunities and access to resources, equal sharing of responsibilities for the family by men and women, and a harmonious partnership between them are critical to their well-being and that of their families as well as to the consolidation of democracy;

16. Eradication of poverty based on sustained economic growth, social development, environmental protection and social justice requires the involvement of women in economic and social development, equal opportunities and the full and equal participation of women and men as agents and beneficiaries of people-centered sustainable development;

17. The explicit recognition and reaffirmation of the right of all women to control all aspects of their health, in particular their own fertility, is basic to their empowerment;

18. Local, national, regional and global peace is attainable and is inextricably linked with the advancement of women, who are a fundamental force for leadership, conflict resolution and the promotion of lasting peace at all levels;

19. It is essential to design, implement and monitor, with the full participation of women, effective, efficient and mutually rein-

forcing gender-sensitive policies and programs, including development policies and programs, at all levels that will foster the empowerment and advancement of women;

20. The participation and contribution of all actors of civil society, particularly women's groups and networks and other nongovernmental organizations and community-based organizations, with full respect for their autonomy, in cooperation with Governments, are important to the effective implementation and follow-up of the Platform for Action;

21. The implementation of the Platform for Action requires commitment from Governments and the international community. By making national and international commitments for action, including those made at the Conference, Governments and the international community recognize the need to take priority action for the empowerment and advancement of women.

40

JENNIFER BAUMGARDNER AND AMY RICHARDS

A Day without Feminism

2000

The twenty-first century began with a resurgence of feminist activism among young women in the United States. Experiencing a world vastly altered from when their mothers and grandmothers came of age, they faced new quandaries. How would they use their unprecedented sexual freedom? How could they achieve balanced lives in a society that now considers female careers to be normal but still provides little support for parenting? How should they address the growing economic inequality among women? The authors of this Prologue to the Third Wave classic, Manifesta, *looked back on how the movement had affected their own lives to generate perspective for the challenges ahead.*

Jennifer Baumgardner and Amy Richards, *Manifesta: Young Women, Feminism, and the Future* (New York: Farrar, Straus and Giroux, 2000), 315–21.

We were both born in 1970, the baptismal moment of a decade that would change dramatically the lives of American women. The two of us grew up thousands of miles apart, in entirely different kinds of families, yet we both came of age with the awareness that certain rights had been won by the women's movement. We've never doubted how important feminism is to people's lives—men's and women's. Both of our mothers went to consciousness-raising-type groups. Amy's mother raised Amy on her own, and Jennifer's mother, questioning the politics of housework, staged laundry strikes.

With the dawn of not just a new century but a new millennium, people are looking back and taking stock of feminism. Do we need new strategies? Is feminism dead? Has society changed so much that the idea of a feminist movement is obsolete? For us, the only way to answer these questions is to imagine what our lives would have been if the women's movement had never happened and the conditions for women had remained as they were in the year of our births.

Imagine that for a day it's still 1970, and women have only the rights they had then. Sly and the Family Stone and Dionne Warwick are on the radio, the kitchen appliances are Harvest Gold, and the name of your Whirlpool gas stove is Mrs. America. What is it like to be female?

Babies born on this day are automatically given their father's name. If no father is listed, "illegitimate" is likely to be typed on the birth certificate. There are virtually no child-care centers, so all preschool children are in the hands of their mothers, a baby-sitter, or an expensive nursery school. In elementary school, girls can't play in Little League and almost all of the teachers are female. (The latter is still true.) In a few states, it may be against the law for a male to teach grades lower than the sixth, on the basis that it's unnatural, or that men can't be trusted with young children.

In junior high, girls probably take home ec; boys take shop or small-engine repair. Boys who want to learn how to cook or sew on a button are out of luck, as are girls who want to learn how to fix a car. *Seventeen* magazine doesn't run feminist-influenced current columns like "Sex + Body" and "Traumarama." Instead the magazine encourages girls not to have sex; pleasure isn't part of its vocabulary. Judy Blume's books are just beginning to be published, and *Free to Be . . . You and Me* does not exist. No one reads much about masturbation as a natural activity; nor do they learn that sex is for anything other than procreation. Girls do read mystery stories about Nancy Drew, for whom there is no sex, only her blue roadster and having "luncheon."

(The real mystery is how Nancy gets along without a purse and manages to meet only white people.) Boys read about the Hardy Boys, for whom there are no girls.

In high school, the principal is *a* man. Girls have physical-education class and play half-court basketball, but not soccer, track, or cross country; nor do they have any varsity sports teams. The only prestigious physical activity for girls is cheerleading, or being a drum majorette. Most girls don't take calculus or physics; they plan the dances and decorate the gym. Even when girls get better grades than their male counterparts, they are half as likely to qualify for a National Merit Scholarship because many of the test questions favor boys. Standardized tests refer to males and male experiences much more than to females and their experiences. If a girl "gets herself pregnant," she loses her membership in the National Honor Society (which is still true today) and is expelled.

Girls and young women might have sex while they're unmarried, but they may be ruining their chances of landing a guy full-time, and they're probably getting a bad reputation. If a pregnancy happens, an enterprising gal can get a legal abortion only if she lives in New York or is rich enough to fly there, or to Cuba, London, or Scandinavia. There's also the Chicago-based Jane Collective, an underground abortion-referral service, which can hook you up with an illegal or legal termination. (Any of these options are going to cost you. Illegal abortions average $300 to $500, sometimes as much as $2,000.) To prevent pregnancy, a sexually active woman might go to a doctor to be fitted for a diaphragm, or take the high-dose birth-control pill, but her doctor isn't likely to inform her of the possibility of deadly blood clots. Those who do take the Pill also may have to endure this contraceptive's crappy side effects: migraine headaches, severe weight gain, irregular bleeding, and hair loss (or gain), plus the possibility of an increased risk of breast cancer in the long run. It is unlikely that women or their male partners know much about the clitoris and its role in orgasm unless someone happens to fumble upon it. Instead, the myth that vaginal orgasms from penile penetration are the only "mature" (according to Freud) climaxes prevails.

Lesbians are rarely "out," except in certain bars owned by organized crime (the only businessmen who recognize this untapped market), and if lesbians don't know about the bars, they're less likely to know whether there are any other women like them. Radclyffe Hall's depressing early-twentieth-century novel *The Well of Loneliness* pretty much indicates their fate.

The Miss America Pageant is the biggest source of scholarship money for women. Women can't be students at Dartmouth, Columbia, Harvard, West Point, Boston College, or the Citadel, among other all-male institutions. Women's colleges are referred to as "girls' schools." There are no Take Back the Night marches to protest women's lack of safety after dark, but that's okay because college girls aren't allowed out much after dark anyway. Curfew is likely to be midnight on Saturday and 9 or 10 p.m. the rest of the week. Guys get to stay out as late as they want. Women tend to major in teaching, home economics, English, or maybe a language—a good skill for translating someone else's words. The women's studies major does not exist, although you can take a women's studies course at six universities, including Cornell and San Diego State College. The absence of women's history, black history, Chicano studies, Asian American history, queer studies, and Native American history from college curricula implies that they are not worth studying. A student is lucky if he or she learns that women were "given" the vote in 1920, just as Columbus "discovered" America in 1492. They might also learn that Sojourner Truth, Mary Church Terrell, and Fannie Lou Hamer were black abolitionists or civil-rights leaders, but not that they were feminists. There are practically no tenured female professors at any school, and campuses are not racially diverse. Women of color are either not there or they're lonely as hell. There is no nationally recognized Women's History Month or Black History Month. Only 14 percent of doctorates are awarded to women. Only 3.5 percent of MBAs are female.

Only 2 percent of everybody in the military is female, and these women are mostly nurses. There are no female generals in the U.S. Air Force, no female naval pilots, and no Marine brigadier generals. On the religious front, there are no female cantors or rabbis, Episcopal canons, or Catholic priests. (This is still true of Catholic priests.)

Only 44 percent of women are employed outside the home. And those women make, on average, fifty-two cents to the dollar earned by males. Want ads are segregated into "Help Wanted Male" and "Help Wanted Female." The female side is preponderantly for secretaries, domestic workers, and other low-wage service jobs, so if you're a female lawyer you must look under "Help Wanted Male." There are female doctors, but twenty states have only five female gynecologists or fewer. Women workers can be fired or demoted for being pregnant, especially if they are teachers, since the kids they teach aren't supposed to think that women have sex. If a boss demands sex, refers to his female employee exclusively as "Baby," or says he won't pay her unless she gives him a blow job, she either has to quit or succumb— no pun intended. Women can't be airline pilots. Flight attendants are "stewardesses"—waitresses in the sky—and necessarily female. Sex appeal is a job requirement, wearing makeup is a rule, and women are fired if they exceed the age or weight deemed sexy. Stewardesses can get married without getting canned, but this is a new development. (In 1968 the Equal Employment Opportunity Commission—EEOC—made it illegal to forcibly retire stewardesses for getting hitched.) Less than 2 percent of dentists are women; 100 percent of dental assistants are women. The "glass ceiling" that keeps women from moving naturally up the ranks, as well as the sticky floor that keeps them unnaturally down in low-wage work, has not been named, much less challenged.

When a woman gets married, she vows to love, honor, and obey her husband, though he gets off doing just the first two to uphold his end of the bargain. A married woman can't obtain credit without her husband's signature. She doesn't have her own credit rating, legal domicile, or even her own name unless she goes to court to get it back. If she gets a loan with her husband—and she has a job—she may have to sign a "baby letter" swearing that she won't have one and have to leave her job.

. . . The divorce rate is about the same as it is in 2000, contrary to popular fiction's blaming the women's movement for divorce. However, divorce required that one person be at fault, therefore if you just want out of your marriage, you have to lie or blame your spouse. . . . (Domestic violence isn't a term, much less a crime; women are legally encouraged to remain in abusive marriages.) . . . If a woman is downsized from her role as a housewife (a.k.a. left by her husband), there is no word for being a displaced homemaker. As a divorcee, she may be regarded as a family disgrace or as easy sexual prey. After all, she had sex with one guy, so why not *all* guys?

If a woman is not a Mrs., she's a Miss. A woman without makeup and a hairdo is as suspect as a man with them. Without a male escort she may be refused service in a restaurant or a bar, and a woman alone is hard-pressed to find a landlord who will rent her an apartment. After all, she'll probably be leaving to get married soon, and, if she isn't, the landlord doesn't want to deal with a potential brothel.

Except among the very poor or in very rural areas, babies are born in hospitals. There are no certified midwives, and women are knocked out during birth. Most likely, they are also strapped down and lying down, made to have the baby against gravity for the doctor's convenience. If he has a schedule to keep, the likelihood of a cesarean is also very high. *Our Bodies, Ourselves* doesn't exist, nor does the women's health movement. Women aren't taught how to look at their cervixes, and their bodies are nothing to worry their pretty little heads about; however, they are supposed to worry about keeping their little heads pretty. If a woman goes under the knife to see if she has breast cancer, the surgeon won't wake her up to consult about her options before performing a Halsted mastectomy (a disfiguring radical procedure, in which the breast, the muscle wall, and the nodes under the arm, right down to the bone, are removed). She'll just wake up and find that the choice has been made for her.

Husbands are likely to die eight years earlier than their same-age wives due to the stress of having to support a family and repress an emotional life, and a lot earlier than that if women have followed the custom of marrying older, authoritative, paternal men. The stress of raising kids, managing a household, and being undervalued by society doesn't seem to kill off women at the same rate. Upon a man's death, his beloved gets a portion of his Social Security. Even if she has worked outside the home for her entire adult life, she is probably better off with that portion than with hers in its entirety, because she has earned less and is likely to have taken time out for such unproductive acts as having kids.

Has feminism changed our lives? Was it necessary? After thirty years of feminism, the world we inhabit barely resembles the world we were born into. And there's still a lot left to do.

A Chronology of the
American Women's Movement
(1945–2000)

1945   World War II concludes with Allied victory; most women indus-
       trial workers are let go.

1946   Congress of American Women (CAW) is founded.

1950   Mattachine Society is established to fight discrimination against
       homosexuals.

1955   Daughters of Bilitis is founded in San Francisco.

1960   Student Nonviolent Coordinating Committee (SNCC) is founded
       after lunch counter sit-ins.

1961   AFL-CIO sponsors major conference on the problems of working
       women.

       President's Commission on the Status of Women (PCSW) is
       established.

       Women Strike for Peace builds a national mothers' campaign
       against nuclear war.

1962   Students for a Democratic Society (SDS) issues the Port Huron
       Statement, a manifesto for student activists.

1963   Congress passes the Equal Pay Act (the first federal gender
       equity law since 1920).

       Betty Friedan publishes *The Feminine Mystique*.

       PCSW issues its report, *American Women*.

1964   Civil Rights Act passed; Title VII prohibits discrimination in
       employment, including sex, and sets up Equal Employment
       Opportunity Commission (EEOC).

Special thanks to *Feminist Chronicles: 1953–1993*, by Toni Carabillo, Judith Meuli, and
June Bundy Csida (Los Angeles: Women's Graphics, 1993), for the most comprehensive
time line.

1965   *Griswold v. Connecticut* establishes a constitutional "right to privacy" for married couples seeking access to birth control information.

Phrase *women's liberation* is first coined at an SDS conference.

1966   National Organization for Women (NOW) is founded.

National Welfare Rights Organization (NWRO) is established.

1967   Sexism at student-based National Conference for a New Politics conference in Chicago spurs young feminists to organize apart from men.

NOW organizes a national, multicity day of picketing against the EEOC.

LBJ issues Executive Order 11375, requiring affirmative action for women.

1968   EEOC begins taking sex discrimination seriously.

Women's Equity Action League (WEAL) is founded to address legal and economic issues.

First national Women's Liberation conference is held in Lake Villa, Illinois.

Shirley Chisholm becomes first African American woman elected to Congress.

1969   U.S. Labor Department and Women's Bureau reverse old opposition to the Equal Rights Amendment (ERA).

Chicago activists organize the clinic "Jane"; NARAL (National Association to Repeal Abortion Laws—later National Abortion Rights Action League) is founded.

Stonewall rebellion in Greenwich Village, New York, leads to founding of the Gay Liberation Front.

1970   First issue of *Women and Their Bodies*, precursor to *Our Bodies, Ourselves*, is published.

ACORN (Association of Community Organizations for Reform Now) is founded in Little Rock, Arkansas, by welfare rights veterans.

WEAL files class-action complaint against 350 American colleges and universities to end sex discrimination in higher education and medical schools.

NOW convention divides over lesbianism.

Abortion laws are liberalized in New York, Hawaii, and Alaska.

Women's Strike for Equality is held.

1971   Women's Legal Defense and Education Fund is established.

U.S. Civil Rights Commission creates task force on sex discrimination.

Advocates for Women is founded as the first women's economic development center focusing on needs of low-income women.

Colleges begin offering courses in women's history and literature.

NOW petitions Federal Communications Commission for inclusion of women in affirmative action by broadcast licensees.

National Women's Political Caucus (NWPC) is formed.

First national conference of Chicanas meets in Houston.

1972 Title IX of the Higher Education Act is passed.

ERA passes both houses of Congress; goes to states for ratification.

First rape crisis centers and battered women's shelters open their doors.

First female rabbi is ordained.

National Conference of Puerto Rican Women is founded.

Asian American Women's Center is established in Los Angeles.

Phyllis Schlafly establishes STOP ERA, the first mass antifeminist organization.

Ms. magazine begins publication.

1973 *Roe v. Wade* decriminalizes abortion; National Right to Life Committee is founded.

National Black Feminist Organization is founded.

Women Employed (WE) is founded, launching movement to improve situation of clerical workers (one in three employed women).

Feminists boycott the Farah clothing company in solidarity with the mostly Mexican American women unionists who are on strike.

NOW files first suit against sex-segregated home economics and shop classes.

U.S. Supreme Court outlaws sex-segregated job ads.

AT&T pays largest back-pay settlement in U.S. history—$38 million—to women and minority men for pervasive discrimination documented by the EEOC.

AFL-CIO convention supports ERA for the first time.

American Psychiatric Association ceases classifying homosexuality as a disorder.

1974 Mexican American Legal Defense and Education Fund launches the Chicana Rights Project.

Wave of gender equity lawsuit victories—for example, teachers can no longer be fired for pregnancy; National Little League opened to girls.

Committee to End Sterilization Abuse (CESA) is founded to stop involuntary sterilization of low-income women of color, especially Puerto Ricans.

Eleven women are ordained as Episcopal priests, defying church rules.

Women of All Red Nations is formed by American Indian women.

Coalition of Labor Union Women (CLUW) is created in convention of 3,200 women representing fifty-eight unions with millions of members.

1975   United Nations declares a "Decade for Women."

NOW introduces the phrase *displaced homemakers* and pushes for public policies to support them.

Congress opens U.S. military academies to women.

National Women's Health Network is established to coordinate growing women's health movement.

1976   Congress amends the Civil Rights Act to protect pregnant women from discrimination.

Episcopal Church recognizes ordination of fifteen women priests.

Organization of Pan Asian American Women is founded.

1977   Congress passes Hyde Amendment denying Medicaid funding to poor women who want abortions; first of many restrictions on access.

First National Women's Conference is held in Houston.

National Women's Studies Association is formed.

1978   Congress passes the Pregnancy Discrimination Act.

Four thousand Catholics march in Baltimore to support the ordination of women as priests.

President Carter institutes nationwide affirmative action for women in construction after a feminist lawsuit against the government; women begin entering "nontraditional" blue-collar jobs in significant numbers.

First "Take Back the Night" March is held in Boston.

1979   Jerry Falwell establishes the Moral Majority to oppose abortion, the ERA, and gay rights, and promote conservatism.

Women Against Pornography announces that "pornography is a feminist issue" in a protest in Times Square; conflict grows among antiporn and "pro-sex" feminists.

First National March for Lesbian and Gay Rights attracts over 100,000 marchers to Washington, D.C.

1980 Gender integration of the armed forces begins.

1981 In San Jose, California, the public workers' union AFSCME wages the first winning strike for equal pay for women for work of comparable value.

Sandra Day O'Connor becomes the first woman U.S. Supreme Court justice.

1982 ERA fails for lack of ratification by enough states.

1983 Washington State women workers win landmark "comparable worth" decision.

1984 U.S. congresswoman Geraldine Ferraro (D-NY) is the first major-party female vice-presidential candidate.

1985 Clerical workers at Yale University win a major victory in a strike for pay equity.

1986 Supreme Court rules in *Meritor Savings Bank, FSB v. Vinson* that sexual harassment on the job is discrimination.

NOW-sponsored March for Women's Lives is held in Washington, D.C.

Congress passes stricter rape laws and ends exemption that allowed marital rape.

Congress designates March as Women's History Month.

1988 U.S. Catholic bishops issue pastoral letter calling sexism a sin.

Operation Rescue is organized to shut down abortion clinics; pro-choice activists organize clinic defenses.

1989 NOW organizes largest rally in Washington, D.C., history.

Supreme Court's *Webster's* decision upholds some state restrictions on abortion.

1990 Women's Environment and Development Organization, a global NGO, is founded by former congresswoman Bella Abzug.

1991 Senate holds public hearings on allegations that Supreme Court nominee Clarence Thomas sexually harassed attorney Anita Hill at EEOC; Thomas is confirmed.

Seven hundred college and high school students attend NOW's Young Feminist Conference in Akron, Ohio.

1992 NOW celebrates its twenty-fifth anniversary with a Global Feminism Conference.

Freedom Summer '92, the inaugural project of the Third Wave Foundation, enlists 120 activists who register over 20,000 new voters.

1993 Ruth Bader Ginsburg, former head of the ACLU Women's Rights Project, becomes U.S. Supreme Court justice.

Global Campaign for Women's Human Rights (950 member groups from numerous nations) becomes powerful lobby at Vienna United Nations World Conference on Human Development.

UN Human Development Report concludes that despite many changes "women are the world's largest excluded group."

1994 Congress passes the Violence Against Women Act.

1995 UN World Women's Conference is held in Beijing, China.

2000 *Manifesta: Young Women, Feminism, and the Future*, by Jennifer Baumgardner and Amy Richards, brings the message of Third Wave feminism to a wide readership.

Questions for Consideration

1. What social changes in the postwar years opened women to feminism's message?
2. What role did the New Deal and World War II experiences play in setting the stage for an upsurge of the women's movement?
3. How did feminists, initially a small minority of the population, win sweeping changes so quickly in the late 1960s and early 1970s?
4. In what ways did the women's movement alter mainstream American culture and institutions?
5. What did the slogan "the personal is political" mean, and why did it prove important?
6. Why did the movement take on so many issues on so many fronts?
7. In what ways did the conflicts among women with different backgrounds and views hurt the cause? In what ways did they advance it?
8. What kinds of changes do you feel must still be made for meaningful equality for women? Why?
9. Looking over the varied strands of the movement, which approaches do you believe were most successful, and why?
10. How does the feminist movement compare to other social movements you may have studied, such as the abolition movement, the labor movement, the civil rights movement, or the gay and lesbian rights movement? How do you explain the similarities and differences?

Selected Bibliography

Note: the article literature is too vast for citation here; it can be found through database searches.

SECONDARY LITERATURE

Bailey, Beth. *Sex in the Heartland*. Cambridge, Mass.: Harvard University Press, 1999.

Baumgardner, Jennifer, and Amy Richards. *Manifesta: Young Women, Feminism, and the Future*. New York: Farrar, Straus and Giroux, 2000.

Breines, Wini. *Young, White, and Miserable: Growing Up Female in the Fifties*. Boston: Beacon Press, 1992.

———. *The Trouble between Us: An Uneasy History of White and Black Women in the Feminist Movement*. New York: Oxford University Press, 2006.

Boyd, Nan Alamilla. *Wide-Open Town: A History of Queer San Francisco to 1965*. Berkeley: University of California Press, 2003.

Brownmiller, Susan. *In Our Time: Memoir of a Revolution*. New York: Dial Press, 1999.

Carabillo, Toni, Judith Meuli, and June Bundy Csida. *Feminist Chronicles: 1953–1993*. Los Angeles: Women's Graphics, 1993.

Chafe, William H. *The American Woman: Her Changing Social, Economic, and Political Roles, 1920–1970*. New York: Oxford University Press, 1972.

Clendinen, Dudley, and Adam Nagourney. *Out for Good: The Struggle to Build a Gay Rights Movement in America*. New York: Touchstone, 1999.

Cobble, Dorothy Sue. *The Other Women's Movement: Workplace Justice and Social Rights in Modern America*. Princeton, N.J.: Princeton University Press, 2004.

Collins, Patricia Hill. *Black Feminist Thought: Knowledge, Consciousness, Empowerment*. Boston: Unwin Hyman, 1990.

Cook, Blanche Wiesen. *Eleanor Roosevelt*. New York: Viking, 1992.

Coontz, Stephanie. *Marriage, a History: From Obedience to Intimacy*. New York: Viking, 2005.

Cott, Nancy F. *The Grounding of Modern Feminism*. New Haven, Conn.: Yale University Press, 1987.

Crawford, Vicki L., et al., eds. *Women in the Civil Rights Movement: Trailblazers and Torchbearers, 1941–1965.* Bloomington: Indiana University Press, 1990.

Davis, Angela. *Women, Race and Class.* New York: Random House, 1981.

D'Emilio, John, and Estelle B. Freedman. *Intimate Matters: A History of Sexuality in America.* New York: Harper & Row, 1988.

Deslippe, Dennis A. *"Rights, Not Roses": Unions and the Rise of Working-Class Feminism, 1945–1980.* Urbana: University of Illinois Press, 2000.

Douglas, Susan J. *Where the Girls Are: Growing Up Female with the Mass Media.* New York: Times Books, 1994.

Echols, Alice. *Daring to Be Bad: Radical Feminism in America, 1967–1975.* Minneapolis: University of Minnesota Press, 1989.

Ehrenreich, Barbara. *The Hearts of Men: American Dreams and the Flight from Commitment.* New York: Anchor Books, 1983.

Enke, Anne. *Finding the Movement: Sexuality, Contested Space, and Feminist Activism.* Durham, N.C.: Duke University Press, 2007.

Evans, Sara M. *Personal Politics: The Roots of Women's Liberation in the Civil Rights Movement and the New Left.* New York: Alfred A. Knopf, 1979.

———. *Tidal Wave: How Women Changed America at Century's End.* New York: Free Press, 2003.

Ezekiel, Judith. *Feminism in the Heartland.* Columbus: Ohio State University Press, 2002.

Faderman, Lillian. *Odd Girls and Twilight Lovers: A History of Lesbian Life in Twentieth-Century America.* New York: Columbia University Press, 1991.

Faludi, Susan. *Backlash: The Undeclared War against American Women.* New York: Crown, 1991.

Fehn, Bruce. *Striking Women: Gender, Race and Class in the United Packinghouse Workers of America.* Iowa City: University of Iowa Press, 2003.

Ferree, Myra Marx, and Beth B. Hess. *Controversy and Coalition: The New Feminist Movement.* Boston: Twayne, 1985.

Ferree, Myra Marx, and Patricia Yancey Martin. *Feminist Organizations: Harvest of the New Women's Movement.* Philadelphia: Temple University Press, n.d.

Freedman, Estelle B. *No Turning Back: The History of Feminism and the Future of Women's Liberation.* New York: Ballantine Books, 2002.

Freeman, Jo. *The Politics of Women's Liberation: A Case Study of an Emerging Social Movement and Its Relation to the Policy Process.* New York: David McKay, 1975.

Gabin, Nancy F. *Feminism in the Labor Movement: Women and the United Auto Workers, 1935–1975.* Ithaca, N.Y.: Cornell University Press, 1990.

Gallo, Marcia M. *Different Daughters: A History of the Daughters of Bilitis and the Rise of the Lesbian Rights Movement.* New York: Carroll & Graf, 2006.

Giddings, Paula. *When and Where I Enter: The Impact of Black Women on Race and Sex in America*. New York: William Morrow, 1984.

Gilmore, Stephanie, ed. *Feminist Coalitions: Historical Perspectives on Second-Wave Feminism in the United States*. Urbana: University of Illinois Press, 2008.

Gordon, Linda. *Woman's Body, Woman's Right: A Social History of Birth Control in America*, Rev. Ed. New York: Penguin, 1990.

Greene, Christina. *Our Separate Ways: Women and the Black Freedom Movement in Durham, North Carolina*. Chapel Hill: University of North Carolina Press, 2005.

Gutiérrez, Elena. *Fertile Matters: The Politics of Mexican-American Women's Reproduction*. Austin: University of Texas Press, 2008.

Harrison, Cynthia. *On Account of Sex: The Politics of Women's Issues, 1945–1968*. Berkeley: University of California Press, 1988.

Hartmann, Susan M. *From Margin to Mainstream: American Women and Politics since 1960*. New York: Alfred A. Knopf, 1989.

———. *The Other Feminists: Activists in the Liberal Establishment*. New Haven, Conn.: Yale University Press, 1998.

Harvey, Brett. *The Fifties: A Women's Oral History*. New York: Harper-Collins, 1993.

Herr, Lois Kathryn. *Women, Power, and AT&T: Winning Rights in the Workplace*. Boston: Northeastern University Press, 2003.

Hooks, Bell. *Ain't I a Woman: Black Women and Feminism*. Boston: South End Press, 1981.

———. *Feminist Theory from Margin to Center*. Boston: South End Press, 1984.

———. *Talking Back: Thinking Feminist, Thinking Black*. Boston: South End Press, 1989.

Horowitz, Daniel. *Betty Friedan and the Making of "The Feminine Mystique": The American Left, the Cold War, and Modern Feminism*. Amherst: University of Massachusetts Press, 1998.

Isenberg, Nancy. *Sex and Citizenship in Antebellum America*. Chapel Hill: University of North Carolina Press, 1998.

Johnson, David K. *The Lavender Scare: Gays and Lesbians in the Federal Government*. Chicago: University of Chicago Press, 2004.

Kaplan, Laura. *The Story of Jane: The Legendary Underground Feminist Abortion Service*. Chicago: University of Chicago Press, 1995.

Katzenstein, Mary Fainsod. *Faithful and Fearless: Moving Feminist Protest inside the Church and Military*. Princeton, N.J.: Princeton University Press, 1998.

Kennedy, Elizabeth Lapovsky, and Madeline D. Davis. *Boots of Leather, Slippers of Gold: The History of a Lesbian Community*. New York: Routledge, 1993.

Kessler-Harris, Alice. *Out to Work: A History of Wage-Earning Women in the United States*. New York: Oxford University Press, 1982.

Klatch, Rebecca E. *Women of the New Right*. Philadelphia: Temple University Press, 1987.

Lee, Chana Kai. *For Freedom's Sake: The Life of Fannie Lou Hamer*. Urbana: University of Illinois Press, 1999.

Lerner, Gerda. *Creation of Feminist Consciousness: From the Middle Ages to Eighteen-Seventy*. New York: Oxford University Press, 1993.

Luker, Kristin. *Abortion and the Politics of Motherhood*. Berkeley: University of California Press, 1984.

Lynn, Susan. *Progressive Women in Conservative Times: Racial Justice, Peace, and Feminism, 1945 to the 1960s*. New Brunswick, N.J.: Rutgers University Press, 1992.

MacLean, Nancy. *Freedom Is Not Enough: The Opening of the American Workplace*. Cambridge, Mass.: Harvard University Press, 2006.

Mansbridge, Jane J. *Why We Lost the ERA*. Chicago: University of Chicago Press, 1986.

Matthews, Donald G., and Jane Sherron De Hart. *Sex, Gender, and the Politics of the ERA: A State and the Nation*. New York: Oxford University Press, 1990.

May, Elaine Tyler. *Homeward Bound: American Families in the Cold War Period*. New York: Basic Books, 1988.

Meyerowitz, Joanne. *Not June Cleaver: Women and Gender in Postwar America*. Philadelphia: Temple University Press, 1994.

Murray, Pauli. *Pauli Murray: The Autobiography of a Black Activist, Feminist, Lawyer, Priest, and Poet*. Knoxville: University of Tennessee Press, 1989.

Nadasen, Premilla. *Welfare Warriors: The Welfare Rights Movement in the United States*. New York: Routledge, 2005.

Nelson, Jennifer. *Women of Color and the Reproductive Rights Movement*. New York: New York University Press, 2003.

Orleck, Annelise. *Storming Caesar's Palace: How Black Mothers Fought Their Own War on Poverty*. Boston: Beacon Press, 2005.

Petchesky, Rosalind Pollack. *Abortion and Woman's Choice: The State, Sexuality, and Reproductive Freedom*. Boston: Northeastern University Press, 1990.

Ransby, Barbara. *Ella Baker and the Black Freedom Movement: A Radical Democratic Vision*. Chapel Hill: University of North Carolina Press, 2003.

Reagan, Leslie. *When Abortion Was a Crime: Women, Medicine, and Law in the United States, 1867–1973*. Berkeley: University of California Press, 1997.

Robinson, Jo Ann Gibson, with David J. Garrow. *The Montgomery Bus Boycott and the Women Who Started It: The Memoir of Jo Ann Gibson Robinson*. Knoxville: University of Tennessee Press, 1987.

Rosen, Ruth. *The World Split Open: How the Modern Women's Movement Changed America*. New York: Viking, 2000.

Roth, Benita. *Separate Roads to Feminism: Black, Chicana, and White Feminist Movements in America's Second Wave.* New York: Cambridge University Press, 2004.

Ruiz, Vicki L. *Cannery Women, Cannery Lives: Mexican Women, Unionization, and the California Food Processing Industry, 1930–1950.* Albuquerque: University of New Mexico Press, 1987.

———. *From Out of the Shadows: Mexican Women in Twentieth-Century America.* New York: Oxford University Press, 1998.

———, and Ellen Carol DuBois. *Unequal Sisters: A Multicultural Reader in U.S. Women's History,* 2nd ed. New York: Routledge, 1994.

Rupp, Leila, and Verta Taylor. *Survival in the Doldrums: The American Women's Rights Movement, 1945 to the 1960s.* New York: Oxford University Press, 1987.

Silliman, Jael, et al. *Undivided Rights: Women of Color Organize for Reproductive Choice.* Boston: South End Press, 2004.

Snitow, Ann, Christine Stansell, and Sharon Thompson. *Powers of Desire: The Politics of Sexuality.* New York: Monthly Review, 1983.

Solinger, Rickie. *Wake Up Little Susie: Single Pregnancy and Race before Roe v. Wade.* New York: Routledge, 1992.

Springer, Kimberly. *Living for the Revolution: Black Feminist Organizations, 1968–1980.* Durham, N.C.: Duke University Press, 2005.

Tait, Vanessa. *Poor Workers' Unions: Rebuilding Labor from Below.* Boston: South End Press, 2005.

Wandersee, Winifred D. *On the Move: American Women in the 1970s.* Boston: Twayne, 1988.

White, Deborah Gray: *Too Heavy a Load: Black Women in Defense of Themselves, 1894–1994.* New York: W. W. Norton, 1998.

PRIMARY SOURCE COLLECTIONS

Asian Women United of California, eds. *Making Waves: An Anthology of Writings by and about Asian American Women.* Boston: Beacon Press, 1989.

Baxandall, Rosalyn, Linda Gordon, and Susan Reverby, eds. *America's Working Women: A Documentary History.* New York: Vintage Books, 1976.

Baxandall, Rosalyn, and Linda Gordon, eds. *Dear Sisters: Dispatches from the Women's Liberation Movement.* New York: Basic Books, 2000.

Garcia, Alma M. *Chicana Feminist Thought: The Basic Historical Writings.* New York: Routledge, 1997.

Guy-Sheftall, Beverly, ed. *Words on Fire: An Anthology of African-American Feminist Thought.* New York: The New Press, 1995.

Howard, Angela, and Sasha Ranae Adams Tarrant, eds. *Anti-Feminism in America: A Collection of Readings from the Literatures of Opponents to U.S. Feminism, 1948 to the Present.* New York: Garland Press, 1997.

Jay, Karla, and Allen Young. *Out of the Closets: Voices of Gay Liberation.* New York: Douglas, 1972.

Kimmel, Michael S., and Thomas Mosmiller. *Against the Tide: Pro-Feminist Men in the United States, 1776–1990.* Boston: Beacon Press, 1992.

Keetley, Dawn Elizabeth, and John Charles Pettegrew, eds. *Public Women, Public Words: A Documentary History of American Feminism*, Vol. III. Madison, Wisc.: Madison House, 1997.

Langley, Winston E., and Vivian C. Fox. *Women's Rights in the United States: A Documentary History.* Westport, Conn.: Greenwood Press, 1994.

Lerner, Gerda. *Black Women in White America: A Documentary History.* New York: Vintage, 1972.

———. *The Female Experience: An American Documentary.* New York: Oxford University Press, 1991.

Michel, Sonya, and Robyn Muncy. *Engendering America: A Documentary History, 1865 to the Present.* New York: McGraw-Hill, 1999.

Moraga, Cherríe, and Gloria Anzaldúa, eds. *This Bridge Called My Back: Writings by Radical Women of Color.* Watertown, Mass.: Persephone Press, 1981.

Morgan, Robin, ed. *Sisterhood Is Powerful: An Anthology of Writings from the Women's Liberation Movement.* New York: Vintage Books, 1970.

O'Farrell, Brigid, and Joyce L. Kornbluh. *Rocking the Boat: Union Women's Voices, 1915–1975.* New Brunswick, N.J.: Rutgers University Press, 1996.

Papachristou, Judith. *Women Together: A "Ms." Book.* New York: Alfred A. Knopf, 1976.

Seifer, Nancy. *"Nobody Speaks for Me!": Self-Portraits of American Working Class Women.* New York: Simon and Schuster, 1976.

Sigerman, Harriet, ed. *The Columbia Documentary History of American Women since 1941.* New York: Columbia University Press, 2003.

Skinner, Ellen. *Women and the National Experience: Primary Sources in American History.* Boston: Addison-Wesley, 1996.

Smith, Barbara. *Home Girls: A Black Feminist Anthology.* New York: Kitchen Table—Women of Color Press, 1983.

Strom, Sharon Hartman. *Women's Rights.* Westport, Conn.: Greenwood Press, 2003.

Williams, Walter L., and Yolanda Retter. *Gay and Lesbian Rights in the United States: A Documentary History.* Westport, Conn.: Greenwood Press, 2003.

Acknowledgments (continued from p. iv)

Document 2. Edith M. Stern, "Women Are Household Slaves," *The American Mercury* 68, no. 301 (January 1949): 71–76. © by Legion for the Survival of Freedom, Inc. Reprinted with permission.

Document 3. Gerda Lerner, "A Union Protects Its Members," from *Proceedings: 15th Annual Convention, UAW-CIO* (1955). Reprinted in Gerda Lerner, *The Female Experience: An American Documentary* (Bobbs-Merrill, 1977). Copyright © 1955 by Gerda Lerner. Reprinted with permission of Stephanie Lerner Lapidus, Trustee of Gerda Lerner Literary Fund.

Document 4. Daughters of Bilitis, "Purpose of Daughters of Bilitis," first published in *The Ladder* (March 1957). Reprinted in *Battered Wives* by Del Martin. Volcano Press edition copyright © 1981. Permission to reprint courtesy of Volcano Press, Inc. www.volcanopress.com.

Document 5. Ella Baker, "Developing Community Leadership," in Gerda Lerner, ed., *Black Women in White America: A Documentary History* (Random House, 1972). Copyright © 1970 by Ella Baker. Reprinted with permission of Carolyn D. Brockington.

Document 6. From Adams, Judith Porter (author), *Peacework: Oral Histories of Women Peace Activists.* © 1991 Gale, a part of Cengage Learning, Inc. Reproduced by permission. www.cengage.com/permissions.

Document 9. National Organization for Women, "Statement of Purpose" (1963), reprinted in *It Changed My Life: Writings on the Women's Movement* by Betty Friedan. Copyright © 1963. Used with permission of Curtis Brown, Ltd.

Document 10. Originally written and distributed in November 1968, then reprinted in *Notes from the Second Year* in 1970, "A Program for Feminist Consciousness Raising" can be found in *Feminist Revolution*, edited by Redstockings (New Paltz, New York, Redstockings, 1975; Abridged Ed. with Additional Writings, New York, Random House, 1978). Information about obtaining this and materials on how women's liberation groups are using consciousness-raising today is available at www.redstockings.org and by mail from Redstockings Women's Liberation Archives for Action, PO Box 744, Stuyvesant Station, NY, NY 10009.

Document 11. Margaret Cerullo, "Hidden History: An Illegal Abortion in 1968," in *From Abortion to Reproductive Freedom: Transforming a Movement*, ed. Marlene Gerber Fried. Copyright © 1990 South End Press. Reprinted with permission.

Document 12. National Organization for Women, "Why Feminists Want Child Care" (1969). Copyright © by National Organization for Women, New York City. Reprinted with permission.

Document 13. Alice de Rivera, "On De-Segregating Stuyvesant High." First published in *Leviathan* magazine, 1969.

Document 15. Gainesville Women's Liberation, "What Men Can Do for Women's Liberation," reprinted in *Dear Sisters: Dispatches from the Women's Liberation Movement*, eds. Rosalyn Baxandall and Linda Gordon. Copyright © 2000 Rosalyn Baxandall and Linda Gordon. Reprinted by permission of Basic Books, a member of the Perseus Books Group.

Document 16. Young Lords Party, "Position Paper on Women" (1970), reprinted in Dear Sisters: Dispatches from the Women's Liberation Movement, eds. Rosalyn Baxandall and Linda Gordon. Copyright © 2000 Rosalyn Baxandall and Linda Gordon. Reprinted by permission of Basic Books, a member of the Perseus Books Group.

Document 17. Patricia Mainardi, "The Politics of Housework" (Redstockings, 1970). Copyright © by Patricia Mainardi. Reprinted with permission.

Document 18. A Women's Health Collective, "The Male-Feasance of Health," *Health/PAC Bulletin*, March 1970. Reprinted with permission of the Heatlh/PAC Digital Archive, healthpacbulletin.org.

Document 19. Susan Griffin, from "Rape is a Form of Mass Terrorism," in *Ramparts* 10, no. 3 (September 1971). Used with permission of the author.

Document 20. Radicalesbians, "The Woman-Identified Woman" (1970). Copyright © 1970 by the Radicalesbians. Reprinted with permission of Ellen Shumsky.

Document 21. Workshop Resolutions from First National Chicana Conference," *Chicanas Speak Out: New Voices of La Raza*, ed. Mirta Vidal. Copyright © 1971 by Pathfinder Press. Reprinted by permission.

Document 22. Johnnie Tillmon, "Welfare is a Woman's Issue," *Ms.*, Spring 1972. Reprinted by permission of *Ms.* magazine, © 1972.

Document 23. Chicago Women's Liberation Union: Hyde Park Chapter, "Socialist Feminism: a Strategy for the Women's Movement" (1972). Reprinted with permission of Ellen Tobey Klass.

Document 24. Phyllis Schlafly, "What's Wrong with Equal Rights for Women?" *The Phyllis Schlafly Report* 5, no. 7 (February 1972). Copyright © by Phyllis Schlafly. Reprinted with permission.

Document 25. "What Do I Do for the Next 20 Years?" by Susan Jacoby. Copyright © 1973 by Susan Jacoby. Originally appeared in *The New York Times Magazine* (June 17, 1973). Reprinted by permission of Georges Borchardt, Inc., on behalf of the author.

Document 26. Margaret Sloan Hunter, "Black Feminism: A Mandate," originally published in *Ms.*, May 1974. Reprinted by permission of *Ms.* magazine, © 1974.

Document 27. Letha Scanzoni, "How to Live with a Liberated Wife," *Christianity Today* 20, no. 18 (June 4, 1976): 6–9. Abridged. Used by permission of the author.

Document 28. Anonymous, "Letter from a Battered Wife," (ca. 1976), from *Battered Wives* by Del Martin. Volcano Press edition copyright © 1981. Permission to reprint courtesy of Volcano Press, Inc. www.volcanopress.com.

Document 29. Deirdre Silverman, "Sexual Harrassment Begins with Hiring Procedures" (1976), reprinted in *Dear Sisters: Dispatches from the Women's Liberation Movement*, eds. Rosalyn Baxandall and Linda Gordon. Copyright © 2000 Rosalyn Baxandall and Linda Gordon. Reprinted by permission of Basic Books, a member of the Perseus Books Group.

Document 30. Combahee River Collective, "A Black Feminist Statement" (1977), reprinted in *Capitalist Patriarchy and the Case for Socialist Feminism*, ed. Zillah R. Eisenstein (1979). Copyright © by Monthly Review Press. Reprinted with permission.

Document 31. From "Against the Tide" by Michael Kimmel. Copyright © 1992 by Michael Kimmel and Thomas Mosmiller. Reprinted with permission of Beacon Press, Boston.

Document 32. Mitsuye Yamada, "Asian Pacific Women and Feminism" (1979), published in the first edition of *This Bridge Called My Back: Writings by Radical Women of Color*. Copyright © by Mitsuye Yamada. Reprinted with permission.

Document 33. Excerpt from *Listen, America!* by Jerry Falwell, copyright © 1980 by Jerry Falwell. Used by permission of Doubleday, an imprint of the Knopf Doubleday Publishing Group, a division of Random House LLC. All rights reserved.

Index